YOUR
HEALTHY
DIVORCE
JOURNEY

YOUR HEALTHY DIVORCE JOURNEY

A Step-by-Step Guide Through
the Process of Divorce

ERICA R. ELLIS, PhD

Redwood Publishing, LLC
Orange County, California

Publisher's Note

This publication is designed to provide accurate and authoritative information in regard to the subject matter covered. It is sold with the understanding that the publisher is not engaged in rendering psychological, financial, legal, or other professional services. If expert assistance or counseling is needed, the services of a competent professional should be sought.

Certain names and identifying characteristics have been changed to protect the identities of those involved.

To order additional copies of this book, please contact the publisher at support@childcentereddivorcejourney.com.

ISBN: 978-1-7348444-0-5 (Paperback)
ISBN: 978-1-7348444-1-2 (eBook: ePub)

Library of Congress Control Number: 2020913804

Cover and Interior designed by Redwood Publishing, LLC

Printed in the United States of America.

Your Healthy Divorce Journey is the culmination of my life-long personal and professional divorce journey. It is dedicated to my parents who loved me deeply yet were imperfect in how they navigated their divorce process. I learned from them how important it is to do divorce well, a lesson which has clearly guided my professional path. It is dedicated to all of my patients whose lives have been impacted by divorce and who have entrusted me with their personal stories and emotional pain so that I could help guide them through their own healthy divorce journeys. Most deeply, it is dedicated to my husband and my son who have taught me about the power of love and family. They have helped to guide me through the final steps of healing and helped me more fully understand and appreciate what it means to be part of a healthy, loving family.

EE

CONTENTS

INTRODUCTION

Divorce can be one of life's most difficult challenges. As you begin this painful journey, you are undoubtedly feeling a wide range of emotions including fear, anger, sadness, confusion, and a general sense of being completely overwhelmed. You are probably feeling like you will never get through this process and are terrified that your children may never recover from it. I do not have the power to make this process less painful for you or your children. I do, however, have the knowledge and expertise to help you navigate your way through this life journey in the best possible way.

When I started thinking about writing this book (and creating the website childcentereddivorcejourney.com), I thought a lot about what unique perspective and value I could potentially add to what already existed. What I discovered is that many of the "experts" authoring these books and sites are people who have either lived through divorce as children or who have gone through their own divorce. Their advice and guidance are based upon their own personal experiences and their desire to help others avoid some of the pain that they themselves have felt. While I, too, have lived through parental divorce, my expertise far exceeds that of personal experience alone. I am a PhD-level licensed psychologist with over thirty years of experience treating children, adults, and families in my busy clinical practice. I have helped hundreds of families work their way through divorce and its aftermath. In addition to my practice, I have also taught at the graduate level, have spoken locally, nationally, and internationally on the topic of children of divorce, and am a frequently quoted expert in the local media on divorce-related matters.

To be fair, I did find a number of other impressive websites developed by mental health professionals (although please be aware that a social worker, family therapist, or counselor does not have the same level of clinical training and expertise as a doctoral-level psychologist like myself). However, nowhere did I find a book or a website created by a practicing psychologist who also has years of experience partnering with matrimonial attorneys as a Collaborative Divorce Coach. Through this role, I have received advanced training in matrimonial law and divorce mediation. I am a member of the International Academy of Collaborative Professionals and the current president of the Collaborative Divorce Association of the Capital

District of New York. Together with my legal colleagues, I have helped many divorcing couples successfully resolve their divorce without having to go to court. This experience has significantly expanded my areas of expertise beyond the psychological/emotional impact of divorce to now include all aspects of the divorce process (i.e., expertise in developing custody plans as well as understanding the concepts and processes involved in the equitable distribution of assets and debt as well as spousal maintenance/child support).

I am now clearer about the unique perspective that I have to share and what the added value is that I can provide to you, the reader, through this book and my website (child-centereddivorcejourney.com). I will share with you my vast knowledge about human relationships, including marriages, and what contributes to them lasting and ending. I will help you explore the potential reasons for pursuing a divorce and whether there are options for saving your marriage. If you are ready to initiate a divorce, I will help you understand the various divorce options and the pros and cons of each. I will walk you through all of the steps in a divorce and what each step involves. I will help you make child-centered custody decisions that best protect your children, guide you through the difficult task of talking to your child about an impending divorce, and help you best support your child's emotional needs (as well as your own) as your family navigates through this difficult journey. I will help you develop the skills to effectively co-parent with your ex-spouse in order to avoid any further emotional damage to your child and enhance their quality of life. I will advise you about the when/how of introducing a new significant other to your child so as to minimize the chances of any further pain or loss. And, finally, I will help you navigate the challenging process of creating a new blended family. One thing that I will not do is give you legal advice. I am not an attorney, nor do I pretend to be one. You should always consult with an attorney regarding any and all legal decisions pertaining to your divorce.

Divorce can be a painful and challenging life journey. It can be done well, but it can also be done very poorly. In my practice, I have seen far too many child and adult patients for whom divorce has been a devastating trauma that negatively impacts their lives for years. However, I also know that divorce has the potential to lead to increased happiness, improved mental health, and healthier relationships for you and your child, despite all of the challenges that it poses. My goal is to help you work your way through your divorce journey, step by step, with an emphasis on your emotional well-being and that of your children, so that you can maximize the chances of having a positive outcome. I look forward to helping you create your own personal healthy divorce journey!

SEVERAL DISCLAIMERS

1) I am not an attorney and I will not be providing you with legal advice. You should always consult with an attorney when making legal decisions about your divorce.

2) Every state has specific legal requirements pertaining to divorce and specific language that applies to the logistics of the divorce process. Some of the terminology that I utilize may be more specific to New York, where I practice. However, I have tried to point out where these differences may apply and to utilize terms that are more generic as well as alternative terms used for the same general concepts in different states.

3) I have shared many divorce-related stories in order to bring to life the concepts that I am describing. While the themes of these stories come from my many years of clinical practice, they are generally not based upon a particular person's life. In the rare instance that they are, names have been changed to protect confidentiality.

1

MY PERSONAL DIVORCE JOURNEY

I was sixteen when my mom told me that my father had been having an affair and that he wanted a divorce. She was devastated and angry and openly shared that with me. My eighteen-year-old brother was leaving for college, so I was left to deal with this family mess on my own. My dad moved out shortly after and continued his relationship with the woman with whom he was having an affair. In fact, he told me that he was in love with her and wanted me to meet her whenever I felt ready to do so. My mom personally knew the woman and did not hesitate to share her negative impressions with me. I hated her before I ever met her and struggled to cope with those feelings for years.

My mom had a very difficult time over the next year and I was her most trusted confidante. She turned to me for comfort and support, and to vent her rage toward my dad. I would hear about legal and financial issues between them and how he was shirking his parental responsibility for me and my brother. Of course, my dad had a totally different perspective on these things and he also did not hesitate to share that with me. I was caught in the middle and often did not know whom to believe.

I avoided meeting my dad's girlfriend for quite a while, but ultimately I had no choice but to do so. She was totally different from my mom and, as I had predicted, I hated her. My dad always wanted to include her in our Saturday visits, and this became a source of conflict between us. He ultimately married her when I was a sophomore in college, and they were together for over forty years until her death several years ago. My mom continued to make her disdain for her clear, and always seemed angry and jealous when I would spend time with her and my dad.

Around this time, I started developing some unusual physical symptoms. I saw numerous doctors, had a variety of tests, and no one was able to come up with an explanation for my symptoms. Amazingly, not one doctor asked about current stressors in my life that might be contributing to the development of these symptoms. My parents were also clearly unaware of the role that stress might be playing. As a result, I

2

was never given the opportunity to get help with the emotional issues that I was clearly struggling to cope with, and which were having a negative impact on my physical well-being.

I was always very athletic, and sports were a huge part of my life. They became my major outlet and primary means of coping with stress. I played a different varsity sport every season and, as a result, spent very little time at home. My best friends were my teammates, so I was supported socially as well. Athletics clearly became my lifeline.

I felt horribly guilty when it was time to leave for college and almost chose to stay home rather than leave my mom alone. To her credit, she pushed me to go away to school which I ultimately decided to do. Every school break posed a challenge in terms of which parent I chose to spend time with. I felt guilty regardless of which parent I chose and spent a lot of emotional energy trying to ensure that my choices resulted in fairness for my parents.

My mom eventually started to heal. She became less emotionally needy, her anger began to decrease, and she started to date. She became involved in a long-term relationship and finally seemed happy again. This took a huge amount of pressure off of me and relieved me of the role of her emotional caretaker. However, the sense of being stuck in the middle of my parents did not go away and continued to be triggered over the years by significant events in my life such as my wedding and the birth of my son.

I decided to become a psychologist and, not surprisingly, to specialize in working with children and families. Immediately upon receiving my PhD, I worked for a year at a residential treatment facility for children and then spent seven years as a staff psychologist on an adolescent unit in a private psychiatric hospital. Through these two positions, I gained a tremendous amount of knowledge and experience about children with serious psychiatric problems. I then decided to establish my own practice and have been seeing patients in this practice for almost thirty years. I became professionally dedicated to helping my patients more successfully navigate their way through difficult life transitions than I was helped to do. Working with children of divorce has always been my passion. When I learned about the Collaborative Divorce process, I knew that this was a divorce option that could help prevent much of the damage done to children through the nasty litigation process, and I knew that I had to become a part of it. I also developed a Co-Parenting Consultation Service as part of my practice that is aimed at helping separated parents learn how to most effectively co-parent their children. I was, and continue to be, committed to helping children and their families work their way through the divorce process in the best possible way.

Given my belief that all psychologists should engage in their own therapy, I saw a therapist and worked through many of my unresolved issues related to my parents' divorce. This experience not only helped me heal some of the lingering wounds from my childhood, but also helped me to better understand the experience of being a patient. This work also allowed me to be a healthier partner in my own relationship. I married after finishing my doctorate, have been happily married for thirty years, and we have an adult son who is the greatest joy of my life.

My mom is now ninety-one and has been happily re-married for twenty-four years, and my dad recently passed at age ninety-three. Last Thanksgiving was the first time since their divorce forty-five years ago that we shared a family holiday meal together. My elderly parents hugged when they saw each other and then sat together for hours at my brother's dining room table sharing old memories. It was a long and sometimes painful journey, but this momentous day was reflective of how far we had all finally come. It was truly a moment of healing for me.

My goal is to prevent you from making many of the mistakes that my parents and many of the parents that I have worked with in my practice have made in their divorce journey. I want to help you maximize the chances of this healing taking place much earlier in your and your children's journey.

2

QUESTIONS TO ASK YOURSELF IF YOU ARE IN AN UNHAPPY MARRIAGE

1) Am I in a marriage that is physically or emotionally abusive?

2) Have we done everything possible to save the marriage?

3) Is this my own issue and is there something I can do to fix it?

4) Should we stay together for the sake of the children?

5) Will my children ever recover if we decide to divorce?

AM I IN A MARRIAGE THAT IS PHYSICALLY OR EMOTIONALLY ABUSIVE?

When I first met Dave, he showered me with attention and expensive gifts. He wanted to spend every waking hour with me, and it made me feel like the most important person in the world. He was jealous of time I spent with friends or attention I received from other men, but this just seemed to prove to me how much he liked me and wanted to be with me. As the relationship progressed, there were other signs of him trying to control me, but this always got overshadowed by how special he made me feel. After a year, he proposed, and we married several months later.

This is when things really started to get ugly. Dave started trying to control my every move. He became enraged one night when I told him that I had made plans to have dinner with my best friend. I had never seen this level of anger before and it really scared me. I agreed to cancel my dinner plans with my friend, and I saw her less and less as time went on. Several months later, I had to travel out of town for work and one of my male co-workers was going to be traveling with me. Dave totally flipped out, accusing me of having an affair with him. It seemed as if he had totally lost his mind but there was no convincing him that he was being irrational. When I tried to explain that I couldn't get out of the trip he hit me for the first time. I felt as if my world was crumbling down around me! He spent the next week apologizing, sending me flowers, and promising that it would never happen again. I desperately wanted to believe him, and I tried to focus on the wonderful parts of him that I still loved.

Of course, this was only the first of many episodes of physical abuse. His anger, jealousy, and suspiciousness frequently surfaced, and I was regularly accused of cheating on him. He constantly checked my phone and computer for evidence, which of course he never found. He became demeaning and belittling, screaming that no one else would be interested in such a loser like me. I started to believe him! I felt trapped in this miserable relationship but felt like it was my only option since he was the only person that would ever love me.

When our son Brandon was born, things deteriorated even further. Dave was now jealous of the attention that I gave to the baby and he was in a constant state of rage. The physical abuse increased in frequency and intensity. I had to avoid my family for fear of them seeing the bruises on my face. My world got smaller and smaller and I got more and more depressed. I felt lost, powerless, and hopeless, and didn't know what to do.

As a psychologist, it is actually quite rare to tell a patient exactly what they should do in a particular situation. Usually my role is to help someone identify their options, weigh those options, and then help them make the choice that works best for them. However, if you are living in an abusive relationship (either toward yourself or your children), my advice is always clear and direct: get out and get out quickly!

If you are uncertain whether your relationship is abusive, ask yourself whether your spouse is:

- Possessive
- Jealous
- Threatening
- Physically violent
- Controlling
- Blaming
- Isolating
- Demeaning
- Shaming
- Unfaithful

If you are still uncertain, ask yourself whether your relationship results in you feeling:

- Badly about yourself
- Scared
- Intimidated
- Vulnerable
- Trapped
- Depressed
- Like you are constantly walking on eggshells

If these descriptions apply to your spouse's behavior or to how you feel when you are with him or her, please be honest with yourself and accept the fact that you are living in an abusive relationship. You do not have the power to change anyone other than yourself and these behaviors will not magically go away, despite all of the promises that are made to you to the contrary. Changing these patterns of behavior is possible, but not without a lot of professional help and hard work. Please also be clear that your spouse's positive qualities do not negate the abusive ones. No one should ever have to accept being abused!

Your only sensible option is to physically remove yourself from your abusive spouse. Find a safe place to live with family, friends, or in a community shelter until you have time to find a more permanent living situation. If you are afraid for your safety, go to your local police station and file a report to request a Restraining/Personal Protection Order that requires your spouse to have no contact with you. Contact a national or local Domestic Violence agency (the phone number for the National Domestic Violence Hotline is 1-800-799-7233) to get support and practical suggestions regarding your legal options. Find a therapist to help you cope with all of the emotions that you are experiencing. If your spouse is not willing to commit to the hard work involved in changing a longstanding pattern of abuse, then your only safe option is to end your marriage. You and your children deserve to be safe, to be treated with dignity and respect, and to not live in fear. Please believe that and take the necessary steps to make it happen.

HAVE WE DONE EVERYTHING POSSIBLE TO SAVE THE MARRIAGE?

Frank and Jean have been married for five years and they have a three-year-old daughter, Jennifer. Prior to the birth of their daughter, they had a wonderful marriage.

They shared a lot of common interests, were able to talk about everything, and had a common set of values about money, religion, family, and raising children. They both had careers that they loved and had a large group of supportive friends. They established a system of taking care of household responsibilities that seemed fair and equitable to both of them.

Once their daughter Jennifer was born, they struggled to find a new balance in their life. Jean was on maternity leave for three months which put her in the role of primary caretaker of the baby. Frank expected that she would also take care of all of the household responsibilities since he was working, and she was not. However, she felt that caring for Jennifer was her full-time job and that Frank should continue doing the things that he used to do. They never found the time to talk about this and negotiate an agreement that felt fair to both of them.

While Jean loved the time home with the baby, she terribly missed the adult interactions with her co-workers, and she started to resent the full-time role of housewife. When Frank came home from work, she would either feel angry and resentful or she would be desperate for adult conversation with him. Frank, in turn, would either feel angry with the way she was treating him or overwhelmed with how he felt she was pouncing on him the second he walked in the door. All of these feelings were heightened by his perception of no longer being important to his wife given that all of her time, focus, and affection was directed at Jennifer.

They both became increasingly unhappy and things only got worse once Jean returned to work. She became completely overwhelmed with all of the responsibilities of being Jennifer's primary caretaker in addition to the challenges of her demanding work. They were having a difficult time talking to each other about their feelings and they continued to drift apart. They both started to question whether their marriage was going to survive.

This story is an example of one of the most challenging transitions in any marriage. There are many additional stressors that can affect a marriage and put strains on a relationship. These stressors can be either a positive or a negative change in life circumstance, including:

- Death of a parent or other significant family member
- Serious illness of spouse or another important member of the family
- Loss of job/starting a new job
- Significant change in financial status
- Moving to a new residence

These and other significant life changes, along with the day-to-day challenges of life, can take an emotional toll on any marriage. Some of the ways that this might affect your marriage include:

- Breakdown of communication
- Inability to effectively resolve conflict
- Decrease in emotional and physical intimacy
- Lack of quality time together
- Difficulty making joint decisions

The old adage that "Marriage Takes Work" applies here. If you see these problems developing in your relationship, it does not mean that the marriage is dying but simply that it requires more attention and work. You both need to re-commit to your relationship and put in the time and energy necessary to nurture it. This might involve:

- Establishing a weekly date night

- Setting aside fifteen minutes at the end of every day to turn off the electronics, sit down together, and talk to each other

- Communicate with each other during the day like you used to when you were first dating (i.e., text each other little love notes)

- Agree to tell your spouse something that you appreciate about him/her on a daily basis (i.e., "Thanks for doing the shopping; it really helped me out.")

- During arguments, try to stick to the problem you are arguing about rather than throwing in the last ten things that annoyed you over the past month, and try to avoid blaming and name-calling

If these strategies do not seem to be effective, it might be time to seek professional help. Marital therapy can be extremely useful in helping a couple re-establish healthy patterns of interaction, learn more effective conflict resolution skills, negotiate compromises in areas of disagreement, and more effectively co-parent.

In order for marital therapy to be successful, several assumptions need to be true:
- You both still love each other
- You are both committed to your relationship
- You are both invested in the therapeutic process and the work required
- Neither of you is involved in an extra-marital relationship

If only one of you is invested in healing the relationship, then this process is probably not going to be successful. If neither of you is invested, then the marriage is probably not going to survive. However, if there are children involved, you owe them at least the effort of trying to salvage the relationship. Divorce should always be the last option, not the first.

IS THIS MY OWN ISSUE AND IS THERE SOMETHING I CAN DO TO FIX IT?

Case 1

Becky has struggled with depression for most of her adult life. During the time that she met her future husband,

Dan, she was functioning fairly well. She never talked much with Dan about her mental health issues because she was afraid of scaring him away. Over the next few years while they were dating and after they got married, Becky had several episodes of worsening depression but nothing that she couldn't manage on her own. She continued to hide the extent of her symptoms from her husband for fear that he wouldn't understand or wouldn't want to start a family with her. She then got pregnant and immediately after their daughter Samantha was born, Becky developed extreme postpartum depression.

The extent of her symptoms made it impossible for her to hide it from Dan. She was barely able to function. She was not sleeping well, had almost no appetite, and had no interest in doing anything, including caring for Samantha. She was overwhelmed with anxiety, particularly related to something catastrophic happening to the baby. Dan was terrified about what was happening to his wife but didn't know how to help her. Becky was shutting him out physically and emotionally and wouldn't talk to him about what she was experiencing. It felt like their marriage was falling apart before his eyes.

Case 2

John grew up in a family that was extremely dysfunctional. His father was an alcoholic who would regularly become emotionally and physically abusive towards his mother, his sister, and him. He lived in constant fear of his dad's anger, disapproval, and drunken rage. He tried desperately to be perfect in order to earn his father's approval but felt as if he always fell short. His mother tried to be loving and supportive of John and his sister, but she was often overwhelmed with her own emotional issues rendering her incapable of being there for him and his sister in a consistent way.

As John grew up, he developed a very negative self-image and had a lot of insecurity about himself. It was hard for him to trust people, so he had few friends. He never dated in high school or college because he never believed that he was good enough for anyone to want him as a boyfriend. While he was working in his first job, he met Anne. She initiated the relationship and did most of the pursuing while John struggled to believe that she could ever really be interested in him. Despite his insecurities, the relationship developed, and they eventually got married.

John's trust issues and negative self-image took a toll on their marriage. He struggled to let himself be vulnerable so Anne's attempts to have emotional conversations with him were rarely satisfying. John always felt like Anne was being critical and quickly became defensive when she gave him even the gentlest feedback on anything. John could never fully accept that he was lovable, and that Anne truly loved him, resulting in him often questioning her commitment to their marriage. All of these behaviors pushed Anne further away and got her to the point of questioning whether their marriage could survive.

We all enter a marriage with a complex history of experiences and relationships that determine the person that we are in that marriage. These two scenarios are examples of how someone's individual mental health issues can negatively impact a marital relationship. Neither Becky nor John are bad people, nor are they to blame for their particular problems. However, their individual mental health issues clearly became relationship issues and had a huge impact on their spouses. In order to save their marriages, they each must take the brave step of acknowledging the negative effect that their issues are having on their marriage and then take the even bolder step of seeking treatment for those issues. In addition, their spouses must understand the role that they can play in either supporting them with their issues or making things worse through their own negative reactions. If both spouses don't take these steps, their marriage will probably not survive. If they do receive the therapeutic help that they clearly need, this will give them the best chance of healing their individual and relationship wounds and hopefully save their marriage. I have seen it happen hundreds of times in my practice, so I know that it is possible.

SHOULD WE STAY TOGETHER FOR THE SAKE OF THE CHILDREN?

Beth and Ed have been married for ten years and they have two children, Ben who is nine and Emma who is seven. They have an extremely contentious relationship and frequently have heated arguments in front of the children. The kids often plead with their parents to stop fighting, and at times even try to physically get between them in an attempt to get them to stop. Ben and Emma have both expressed their worry about their parents getting divorced although Beth and Ed try to reassure them that this won't happen. These reassurances are becoming increasingly hard to believe since on many occasions the children have actually heard one parent threatening to divorce the other.

The children have also started to notice that their parents don't seem to like or love each other anymore and are starting to ask questions like:
- *Why aren't you sleeping in the same bed anymore (and they are growing increasingly skeptical about the excuse that dad snores too loudly for mom to sleep)?*
- *Why don't we spend much time together as a family anymore or go on the kinds of vacations that we used to take?*
- *Why does mommy seem sad all of the time?*

- *What have we done that is so bad that you are fighting about us all of the time?*
- *How come you never hug or kiss each other anymore?*
- *What happens to kids when their parents get divorced?*
- *Why is daddy never home anymore?*
- *Why are you two angry all of the time?*
- *Are you going to stop loving us like you stopped loving daddy?*

In addition to asking these types of questions, there has also been a noticeable change in the children's behavior and mood. Ben's teacher has noted that he has become more defiant and bossier and seems to be having a difficult time focusing on his schoolwork. Emma seems sadder and more withdrawn and has been waking up frequently with bad dreams. The parents are attributing these changes to "the kids just going through a stage" and are unable to see the role that their marital difficulties are having on them.

Problems in a marriage can take a significant toll on the children who are forced to witness it. It can have a severe impact on their physical and mental health and interfere in all aspects of their functioning. It also has the potential to negatively affect their own intimate relationships when they become adults. Therefore, staying together for the sake of the children is not a concept that makes sense, and it is rarely a strategy that I suggest to my patients. What does make sense, if at all possible, is committing to working on creating a healthier marital relationship, for the sake of the children. This can involve many steps, including:

- NEVER fighting in front of the children
- Not putting children in the middle of parental conflict
- Seeking professional help in order to improve/save the marriage

There are clearly some marriages that are beyond saving and divorce becomes the only reasonable option. The goal then becomes ending the marriage with the least possible damage being done to the children, as well as to you. It is possible to "do divorce well." That is a much better option than exposing children to constant conflict and turmoil by staying together in a toxic relationship. I know that this is possible, and the rest of this book and childcentereddivorcejourney.com are focused on helping you achieve that goal.

WILL MY CHILDREN EVER RECOVER IF WE DECIDE TO DIVORCE?

Kelsey was six when her parents got divorced. It was a terrifying time for her in so many ways. As is typical for children of that age when parents split, she blamed herself for their divorce. She developed a lot of anxiety around all of the changes and the unpredictability that suddenly defined her life. She had two new homes, had to start a new school, and spent half of her time with each parent so that she was always missing one of them. She hoped that they would get back together despite them frequently telling her that this was not going to happen. She worried that her parents might stop loving her and leave her in the same way that she saw them doing with each other. She felt sad most of the time and worried that she would never feel happy again.

Kelsey's parents knew that all of these feelings were typical of a six-year-old experiencing parental divorce. They were committed to working together to do everything possible to help her cope with this major life change. They found a therapist who specialized in working with children of divorce and got a lot of expert guidance on many things including: how to best tell her about the impending divorce, how to reassure her that she was not responsible for their adult decision, how to maintain as much consistency in her life as possible, how to reassure her of their never ending love, how to tell her/show her they will always work together on her behalf, and how to support her with her painful emotions. They arranged for the therapist to regularly meet with Kelsey as well so as to provide her with a resource to help her cope with every part of her changing life.

Kelsey developed a trusting therapeutic relationship with the therapist and met with her on and off over the course of the next ten years. Sometimes Kelsey met with her alone and sometimes the therapist brought her parents into the sessions to help them talk about things that they were struggling to deal with on their own. Over the years, they got help dealing with issues such as different rules in the two households, each of her parents' dating and ultimate remarriage, the challenges of blended families, and dealing with new half siblings.

While the initial adjustment to the divorce was extremely difficult, Kelsey eventually accepted that this was the new reality of her life and that it wasn't as bad as she had anticipated it would be. Her parents were getting along better than they had before the divorce, and they always worked together on her behalf as they had promised that they would. They were both sensitive to the fact that she missed the parent that she wasn't with and made sure that she was able to speak to both parents on a daily basis. When she complained about how confusing it was to have different rules at the two houses, they worked together to make the rules more consistent. They didn't push their new significant others on her but gave her time to develop a relationship with them at the pace that was comfortable for her. Neither of her parents made her feel guilty about having a relationship with the other parent or their new partner.

As a result of her parents' efforts over the years, Kelsey grew up being a happy, well-adjusted girl. She excelled *academically and was a gifted soccer player. Her parents were her biggest fans, sitting together at every game cheering her on.*

This is not a fantasy scenario, but a realistic story about how resilient children can be and how they can actually thrive in the face of parental divorce. In order for this to happen, the adults need to rise above their own anger and pain and commit to putting their children's needs above their own. This is clearly not an easy task, but it can be done. Every divorcing parent owes it to their child to make this their priority as they make their way through the difficult divorce process. I am here to help you do just that!

3

DIVORCE OPTIONS

Once you have made the difficult decision that you are ready to pursue a divorce, one of the first choices that you will need to make is what type of divorce process you want to utilize. Many people are not aware of the various options available to them and assume that they will need to go to court to resolve their divorce. That is not always the case. In this chapter, I will review the three divorce options, detail the differences between them, and help you better understand what to expect with each of them in order to help you decide which option seems best for you as well as for your children.

MEDIATION

The primary reason that people choose to mediate their divorce is that everything will be negotiated out of court with the help of one professional. This allows the process to be less stressful, take less time, and consequently be less expensive than the other options that are available. There are wide variations across states regarding the exact nature of the mediation process, so it is important for you to research this prior to determining whether this is the right choice for you and your specific situation.

If you choose to mediate your divorce, you and your spouse will typically work with one mediator who is either an attorney or a non-attorney mediator. Utilizing a mediator who is an attorney has numerous benefits. They are usually matrimonial (divorce) attorneys who are highly trained in all of the legal issues pertaining to divorce in your state. In many cases, they are also able to draft and file the final divorce agreement once all decisions have been made; whereas, you would need to hire an attorney to do so if you chose to work with a mediator who is not an attorney. That being said, there are many excellent non-attorney mediators who are highly skilled and effective. Clearly, the most important criteria for choosing a mediator are finding someone 1) whom you feel comfortable with, 2) who has a lot of experience mediating divorces, and 3) who comes highly recommended from trusted sources.

The process of mediation involves sitting together with your spouse and the mediator and negotiating all of the details pertaining to both financial matters and child custody (in some states referred to as Parental Rights or Responsibilities). The mediator does not represent you or your particular interests and is not an advocate for your specific needs. Rather, their role is to facilitate communication, compromise, conflict resolution, and ultimately, agreement on terms. There are also times, particularly in high-conflict situations, that the mediator will separate the spouses and go back and forth between them in an attempt to help them come to an agreement on the terms of the divorce. This is less typical and only utilized under very specific circumstances. There are also situations in which your individual attorneys will be on site during the mediation process so that they are available should a legal consultation become necessary.

Mediation is clearly not for every couple. In order for this process to be successful, several conditions need to apply. First, you generally need to feel safe sitting in the same room as your spouse, and there needs to be a basic level of trust between the two of you. Given that lawyers will not be communicating for you, you need to have a basic ability to communicate with your spouse. You do not need to agree on everything, but you at least need to be able to talk together in order to reach agreement.

There are certain situations that are not well suited to mediation. These include:
- Marriages where there is a history of abuse
- When there has been a total breakdown of trust and/or communication
- When there are highly complicated financial issues (although this is still possible)

- When one or both of the spouses are struggling with substance abuse or serious mental illness (although this is still possible if both spouses can demonstrate a basic level of mental competence)
- If you feel the need to have an attorney who is specifically advocating for your needs

COLLABORATIVE DIVORCE

Collaborative Divorce is the other non-litigated option. This means that both spouses commit to not going to court and to resolve their divorce without engaging in a lengthy and expensive legal battle. It differs from mediation in several important ways. First, both spouses have a collaboratively trained matrimonial attorney who is representing them and specifically advocating for their needs. However, the two collaborative attorneys are not fighting against each other to win (as happens in litigated divorces) but are working towards a mutually created settlement. In addition, one or two collaborative divorce coaches, who are specially trained mental health professionals such as a psychologist or social worker, typically serve as the facilitators of this process. When a single coach is utilized (which is most common), their role is to manage the emotions that inevitably surface during every divorce negotiation and to assure that the communication between spouses remains respectful and productive. Custody decisions are also made with the help of the coach who is able to make sure that the child's particular emotional and age-related needs are the primary basis of those decisions. In the event that there are complicated financial issues that are beyond the expertise of the attorneys, it is also an option to include a Financial Neutral as part of the collaborative team. This person is typically a Certified Divorce Financial Analyst (CDFA) who is specially trained in helping divorcing couples disentangle their finances and creating plans to ensure their financial stability in the future.

The goal of this process is to make decisions about finances and child custody in an atmosphere of respectful communication, honesty, and transparency, and where the needs of the children are always the top priority. It is not a process that is free of conflict, but one in which the conflict is managed toward the goal of negotiating compromise.

There are many benefits to the collaborative process. (In the spirit of full disclosure, let me remind you that I am a collaborative divorce coach and I believe, in most cases, that this is the best possible divorce resolution option available). These include:

- A team of professionals work together to help you negotiate a mutually agreed upon resolution
- You and your spouse learn more effective ways of communicating and resolving conflict that you can utilize going forward as you co-parent with your ex
- As with mediation, you control the process as well as the final decisions that are made (rather than a judge dictating those things)

- There is less stress involved since the professionals are committed to the process and to help you manage your painful emotions
- The multidisciplinary team serves to make this an efficient and cost-effective process compared to litigation which can take much longer and cost significantly more

Should the collaborative process fail, it is important to be aware of the fact that you will need to start all over with new litigation attorneys since your collaborative attorneys will no longer be able to represent you in court. While this poses a significant potential risk, it can also serve to motivate the spouses to see the process through to successful completion.

LITIGATION

The third divorce option is to litigate through the court system. This is a totally different type of process than either mediation or collaborative divorce. Each spouse has an attorney who represents their needs and is committed to fighting for those needs to be met. It is an adversarial process in which the attorneys are working to prove to the judge that their client deserves something (either in terms of money or time with the children) that the other spouse does not deserve. The judge makes the final decision, not the spouses, and that decision is binding.

If you and your spouse are litigating about custody and are unable to reach an agreement, a trial will take place to determine where your child will reside and the schedule of visitation with the other parent. Each lawyer will try to prove why their client having custody is in the best interests of the child. The children will be assigned an attorney (they are referred to differently across states including Attorney for the Child, Counsel for the Minor Child, Law Guardian) who will represent their interests and be their voice in the process. A forensic psychological evaluation of all family members may be completed by a court-appointed psychologist, and the opinion rendered in this evaluation can have significant impact on the judge's ultimate decision.

As you can see from this description of the process, it has the potential to get very ugly very quickly. Accusations will be made about each of you in an attempt to discredit your ability to be a good parent. Your children will be put in the position of feeling like they have to take sides against one of you. All of this serves to increase the tension and anger that typically already exists between you and your spouse, making it increasingly difficult to be able to effectively co-parent with each other in the future.

A litigated divorce can take much longer than the non-litigated options for several reasons. You are at the mercy of the court's calendar which is often crowded and unpredictable. You might have court dates scheduled months apart and post-ponements are not unusual. Evaluations need to be completed and the expert's schedules need to be coordinated with that of the court. Given that we know "time means money," this process can become extremely costly. The attorney's goals are not to work together to negotiate a compromise (as it is in collaborative divorce) but rather to fight to the end on their client's behalf, and this takes time. As is the case for most win-lose battles, both parents and children often pay a high psychological and emotional price. It is rarely ever a win-win proposition.

There are unfortunate circumstances in which litigation is the only option. These include:

- Spouses are unable to reach agreement by means of the non-litigated options
- Domestic violence or abuse is present in the marriage
- One or both spouses are struggling with substance abuse or serious mental illness
- Trust and/or communication have completely broken down between the spouses

If at all possible, resolving your divorce out of court, through either mediation or collaborative divorce, will result in the least amount of emotional turmoil for you and your children. However, there are situations in which litigation is your best option. So, how do you decide which process to choose? I would recommend that you set up meetings with one or more attorneys and explore with them which process they believe would best fit your particular marital situation. Be sure to include attorneys who mediate, collaborate, and litigate so that you can get multiple perspectives on your situation. Based upon their expert opinions, you will have the information necessary to make an informed decision.

4

WHAT DOES A DIVORCE
ACTUALLY ENTAIL?

The Oxford Dictionary defines divorce as "the legal dissolution of a marriage by a court or other competent body." But what exactly happens when you get divorced? What kinds of decisions will you need to make? This chapter will help explain the three major components of every divorce settlement so that you better understand what the process actually entails. I will also introduce you to the legal terms and language of divorce so that they are familiar to you when you hear them in the future. It is important to note that the terminology may be different from state to state but the general principles will be the same regardless of where you reside. Again, I will remind you that I am not an attorney and that I am not providing you with legal advice. It is important to always consult with a matrimonial attorney regarding all legal issues pertaining to your divorce.

The first thing that I would like to clarify is the concept of "No-Fault Divorce" since this is quite confusing for most people starting a divorce action. By definition, this means that neither spouse is required to prove fault or marital misconduct (such as infidelity or abuse) on the part of the other spouse. One spouse must simply assert incompatibility or irreconcilable differences. All states at this time have some version of no-fault divorce. California was the first to pass no-fault legislation in 1970 and New York was the last to do so in 2010. As a result, no matter where you live, you can get a divorce by simply claiming that your marriage is over. It is no longer necessary to prove that your spouse caused the breakup. However, there are variations across states regarding other requirements (such as having to be separated for a specified period of time before being able to divorce or having the option to file on traditional fault grounds). It is therefore imperative that you consult with a divorce attorney or research the divorce laws in your state in order to familiarize yourself with the specific divorce statutes in your particular state of residence. Please go to our website, childcentereddivorcejourney.com, and click on the Resources link for more specific information about these differences.

The three major components of every divorce settlement are 1) Child Custody/Allocation of Parental Rights (assuming that there are children), 2) Equitable Distribution, and 3) Child Support/Spousal Maintenance.

CHILD CUSTODY/ALLOCATION OF PARENTAL RIGHTS

In every divorce where there are children involved, decisions must be made regarding which parent has legal authority to make important decisions about the children (such as medical, educational, and religious decisions), where the children will reside, and the details of a specific visitation schedule.

Sole Legal vs Joint Legal Custody/Decision Making

Sole legal custody means that one parent has the right and responsibility to make all decisions about the health, education, and welfare of the children. Joint legal custody means that both parents share the right and responsibility to make these decisions for their children. Joint legal custody is generally in the best interest of the children assuming that both parents are able to rise above their issues with each other, communicate effectively, and work together on their children's behalf. It also assumes that they are both competent to assume the responsibilities of making these important decisions. If they are not able to do so, then it makes more sense for one parent to have sole legal custody on their own. The kinds of situations that would make a parent incapable of sharing custody might include serious mental health issues, debilitating medical problems, significant substance abuse, or a history of physical or sexual abuse.

Primary Physical vs Joint Physical Custody/ Parenting Time

Primary physical custody means that children will reside with one parent the majority of the time and the other parent will have agreed-upon visitation rights. Joint physical custody means that each parent will have significant periods of physical custody so that they each have continuing and regular contact with the children. It does not necessarily mean "50/50," as many parents assume, but rather some agreed upon parenting schedule that allows both parents to have a significant and close to equal amount of time with the children. Again, it is generally in the children's best interest for two loving and competent parents to each have regular and frequent amounts of time with their children. The same types of parental issues that would result in the decision for one parent to have sole legal custody would also apply to the need for only one parent to have primary physical custody.

There may be situations where it is determined, typically by the court, that one parent should have the right to see their children but that their judgement or behavior is questionable to the point that these visits need to be supervised by another competent adult. Examples of this might be when a parent has a significant mental health or substance abuse issue or when there have been concerns about physical or emotional abuse that have not been totally proven. In these cases, the court will appoint a supervisor (the other parent, a trusted family member, a professional) who is required to be present when the children spend time with this parent. This serves to assure the children's safety while they continue to have a relationship with that parent.

Mediation and Collaborative Law allow parents to determine which of these legal and physical custody arrangements make the most sense for their particular situation. In litigation, the judge will ultimately hold the power to make those decisions after the course of a trial or via a pre-trial settlement. So, the question is, in part, who do you want making those decisions?

In addition to these custody decisions, you will need to develop a very specific *Parenting Plan* that details such things as:

A **Parenting time schedule** that spells out the exact days/ times that the children will be with each of you and how the transitions between homes will take place.

Holiday schedules that detail who the children will be with on major holidays such as Thanksgiving, Christmas, New Year's Eve, Kwanza, Easter, Passover, Memorial Day, Ramadan, Labor Day, Rosh Hashanah/Yom Kippur, Halloween, Mother's Day, Father's Day.

Vacation schedules that detail where the children will spend Christmas vacation, Spring Break, Easter vacation.

Summer schedule – will it stay the same as the regular school year schedule or change based upon the parents' summer schedules?

Birthdays – where will the children spend their birthdays?

Schedule changes – the process by which changes to the schedule will be made, how far in advance this needs to happen, and whether by text/email/phone call/in writing.

Right of first refusal – This is a plan that details what happens when a parent is unavailable for their regularly scheduled parenting time. It specifies under what circumstances the noncustodial parent must be given first choice to have the children. For example, you can decide that this applies when the custodial parent is going to be away for a certain number of hours or for an overnight. This prevents children from being shuffled around to alternate caretakers and assures that the other parent will always be the first option for care when the regularly scheduled parent is not available.

Parental communication – the process by which parents will communicate with each other (i.e., email, text, phone message).

Parental relocation – how far one parent can move from the other, who is responsible for transporting children between homes if one of you chooses to move out of the area.

I want to talk in more detail about creating the specific parenting schedule. This frequently becomes a controversial topic as parents try to prove to each other and the attorneys/judge why they each believe that they should be entitled to more time with the children. This is not a decision that should be based on emotions or control. Rather, it is a decision that should be based upon the best interest of the children. Assuming again that both spouses are healthy, competent, and loving parents, it is typically in the best interest of the children to spend regular and frequent time with both parents. If that is not the case, that will obviously play a major role in the decisions that will be made regarding the parenting schedule.

The specific way in which this regular contact with both parents is accomplished can vary depending upon the age of the particular children involved. Young children (under the age of eight) should ideally not go more than several days without seeing one of their parents. It is simply too difficult for them to deal with the prolonged absence when they are so young. While frequent transitions between homes is also a challenge, it is less emotionally harmful than children going long stretches of time without contact with one parent.

One of the most common parenting schedules for young children is the 2-2-3. This means that on week one the children are with mom for two nights (Monday and Tuesday), dad for the next two nights (Wednesday and Thursday), and then with mom for the following three nights (Friday, Saturday, and Sunday). On week two, this changes so that the children will be with dad on Monday and Tuesday nights, with mom on Wednesday and Thursday nights, and then with dad on Friday, Saturday, and Sunday nights. This alternating week schedule is to assure that the children do not go more than three days without seeing one of their parents and gives parents with shared physical custody a fairly equal amount of time with the children.

Another common parenting schedule for somewhat older children is the 5-2-2-5. This would entail a more consistent schedule where the children are with mom on Monday and Tuesday, with dad on Wednesday and Thursday, and they then alternate every other Friday through Sunday with each parent. This involves a longer period of time away from each parent so it generally should not be utilized with very young children. It does allow for the weekday schedule to remain consistent from week to week which can be a major benefit.

Older teenagers are more able to manage longer periods of time away from one parent so other parenting plans can reasonably be considered. Spending one week with one parent followed by one week with the other has the potential of reducing the number of transitions between homes for the older child. Adding in a mid-week dinner visit with the non-custodial parent can lessen the impact of the long stretches of time away from a parent that is inherent in this alternating week plan.

While it is important to create a parenting schedule that is tailored to the age of your child, it is even more important to ensure that any plan that you agree upon can be implemented consistently over time. Your goal now is to minimize uncertainty and inconsistency for your children as much as possible given all of the change that they have already had to endure. Parents need to stick to the schedule as closely as possible so that the children can count on it happening in a predictable way. There are few things as painful and emotionally damaging as a young child anxiously awaiting the arrival of a parent who never shows to get them! Please avoid that at all costs!

EQUITABLE DISTRIBUTION

Equitable distribution is the fair (but not necessarily equal) division of marital assets and debt obligations acquired during a marriage. Pre-marital assets (those which you owned prior to the marriage) are generally not part of this negotiation and typically remain the sole property of the spouse that owned them prior to the marriage. There are particular situations where there can be exceptions to this general rule which is why you should always be advised by an attorney when making decisions about equitable distribution.

The first step in any financial distribution negotiation is the full disclosure of everything that you own (houses, retirement savings, bank accounts, investment accounts, businesses, valuable jewelry/artwork, vehicles/boats/campers) and everything that you owe (mortgages, home equity loans, car/ school loans, credit card debt). This is accomplished by each spouse honestly and openly completing a Financial Affidavit or Statement of Net Worth (different states have different terminology) which is the vehicle for detailing those assets and liabilities. Samples of these forms can be found in the Resources link on childcentereddivorcejourney.com or can be obtained from an attorney. This is a sworn and notarized legal document so that there are potential legal consequences for inaccurate reporting.

The other significant part of the Financial Affidavit or Statement of Net Worth is the detailing of each of your current expenses once you are no longer living together. This is accomplished by each of you creating a budget of current and/or anticipated future expenses for yourself and your children. The goal of this process is to determine how much money each of you will require to support yourself and your children in the future. That information is then utilized when negotiating the details of equitable distribution as well as child support and maintenance.

In Mediation and Collaborative Law, decisions about how to divide assets and debt are jointly made by the spouses with the help of the professionals facilitating their settlement. There is a lot of room for creative solutions aimed at helping each of you remain as financially secure as possible and you are totally in control of how those decisions are made. In litigation, the judge will determine how your assets and debts will be divided and the rationale behind that decision will not always appear to be fair or logical to you. You are completely at the mercy of the judge's decisions, which at times may seem to you to be quite arbitrary and perhaps even unfair.

One other aspect of equitable distribution is the division of personal property. This involves dividing up all of the personal possessions that you and your spouse have acquired over the course of your marriage, including such things as furniture, artwork, jewelry, electronics, kitchenware, children's toys/clothes, and lawn equipment. A useful strategy for starting this process is for each of you to make a list of the things that have personal/sentimental meaning to you as well as other items which you hope to keep. After these items are split, it then becomes easier to divide the other possessions that don't have as much emotion connected to them.

This is another task where putting the children's needs ahead of your own should be a priority. You need to ensure that the two homes where the children will be living will be full of their familiar clothes, toys, and other possessions in order to make the transition to a new home(s) more comfortable for them. This will also prevent them from having to be transporting their things from house to house every time they make that transition. Therefore, working together to divide the children's things as equally as possible needs to be of primary concern. Remember, this is about making your children as comfortable as possible. You are doing this for them.

CHILD SUPPORT

Child support is money paid by one parent to the other parent for the purpose of helping to pay for the costs of the child's needs. The amount and duration of support payments is determined by state statute specific to the state where you live at the time of divorce. There are very specific legislatively mandated formulas that allow you to calculate the amount of child support that will be required by law given your particular family situation. The number of years that you will be required to pay child support also varies state by state. In New York, for example, a child is entitled to be supported until the age of twenty-one unless the child is considered to be emancipated by means of being married, in the military, or self-supporting. While the amount of the child support obligation varies according to specific state statutes, some general rules apply. When one parent has primary physical custody, the non-custodial parent must typically pay child support to the custodial parent. When parents share joint physical custody, support obligations are based upon how much each parent earns and the percentage of time the child spends with each parent.

You can find detailed information on your state's child support guidelines and calculations on our website (under the Resources link on childcentereddivorcejourney.com) or through an attorney. In terms of tax implications, child support is considered a "tax-neutral event." This means that such payments are not a deductible expense for the person paying it nor is it considered taxable income for the person receiving it.

It is important to understand that the state statutes for support serve only as a guideline if you are utilizing either Mediation or Collaborative Divorce. You have the freedom and flexibility to modify/adjust the calculations to best suit your particular family situation. However, in litigation, those specific formulas and calculations will determine the amount of support that one spouse is obligated to pay.

The person paying child support is often obligated to provide a means for that support to continue through the emancipation of the children should the parent die before that occurs. This is typically accomplished through the purchase of a life insurance policy by the parent paying the support that has the children or the surviving parent as the beneficiary. The amount of the policy will be for the total amount of child support payments that would be owed from the time of divorce through the termination of the child support obligation. For example, if the parent is to pay $500 per month ($6,000 per year) for ten years until the child turns twenty-one, a ten-year-term life insurance policy with a death benefit of $60,000 would need to be secured so that the total amount of child support would be guaranteed should the parent die prematurely.

Divorcing parents are also obligated to plan for how they will provide for a variety of other necessities for their children including: health insurance, non-reimbursed medical expenses (such as co-pays, deductibles, services not covered by insurance), extra-curricular activities, and childcare. Typically, these are paid on a pro rata basis which means that each parent pays a percentage of those required expenses based upon the proportional difference of their respective salaries. Let me give a specific example that will hopefully make that clearer. Let's say that the wife earns $60,000 per year and the husband makes $40,000 per year. Based upon this difference in their salaries, the wife will then be expected to pay three-fifths of those expenses and the husband will pay two-fifths. This serves to equalize the financial burden of these expenses for each parent and will make paying them more manageable for the spouse that earns less money.

Decisions regarding the way in which future college expenses will be funded are also often part of the child support discussion. It is important to note, however, that in some states the court does not have jurisdiction to determine college expenses. This discussion may seem quite premature if your children are young, but should be considered at the time of divorce in order to avoid future conflict. There are many creative ways to plan for this major future expense. For example, you can both agree to put a certain amount of money into a 529 college savings account on a regular basis for each child. You can agree to both being responsible for the cost of a state school and the children would be required to take out loans or secure financial aid should they choose to attend a more expensive private college. You could also choose to punt this decision down the road with the knowledge that you will need to address it when the time comes for your children to go to college, but I would caution against this. The more you are able to settle now, the less conflict you will have about it in the future. As with most divorce-related decisions, this should always be the goal!

SPOUSAL MAINTENANCE
(also known as Alimony or Spousal Support)

The purpose of spousal maintenance is to help the spouse who earns less money maintain close to the standard of living that both spouses had been accustomed to during the course of the marriage. All states have laws and associated formulas that determine whether and how much maintenance will be paid and for what period of time. Specifics regarding your particular state can be found in the Resources section of childcentereddivorce-journey.com or from your attorney. Several factors are considered in the determination of maintenance payments, including: the length of the marriage, the contribution a spouse made as a stay-at-home parent, potential earning ability of both spouses, and the age and physical/emotional health of both spouses.

In Mediation and Collaborative Divorce, the amount and duration of maintenance can be negotiated based upon the needs of the non-moneyed spouse (the one who earns less) and tailored to their specific situation. For example, if the wife stayed home to raise the children and plans post-divorce to go back to college and pursue a marketable degree, the husband can agree to provide financial support long enough for her to complete her degree and secure a job. In divorce litigation, the judge has a tremendous amount of discretion in awarding maintenance even after considering the various factors that typically go into a support determination. The decision is out of your control, cannot be tailored to your specific needs, and there is no recourse if you are unhappy with the determination.

There was a major change in 2019 to the federal tax law pertaining to spousal maintenance. The new law eliminates the tax deduction for the spouse who is paying maintenance for all agreements made after December 31, 2018. This change results in a greater financial burden to the person paying it since the tax savings from being able to deduct maintenance payments in the past was substantial. In addition, recipients of alimony payments will no longer have to include them in taxable income which will have an impact on the amount of support that they actually have available to them.

I have tried to include a lot of detail about the nuts and bolts of what a divorce actually entails and I can guess that your head must be spinning after reading all of this. However, please remember that this is a process and that you will be guided through this process by a professional who is highly trained and knowledgeable about all of these details. You will not be doing this alone. Trust that you will make it through this challenging part of the divorce journey despite how unlikely that might seem right now.

5

TALKING TO YOUR CHILDREN ABOUT DIVORCE

The two most frequent questions that I get from parents who are about to initiate a divorce process are 1) when should I tell the children? and 2) what exactly should I say to them? This can be an extremely anxiety-provoking conversation to anticipate having and a crucially important one to get right. I have unfortunately seen far too many parents do a horrendous job with this important discussion, and I want to make sure that you do not fall into those same dangerous traps. If you follow these guidelines, I can assure you that it will go as well as possible, and that you will spare your children the pain that these typical mistakes can cause.

WHAT **NOT** TO DO

Debbie and John have been married for fourteen years and have two children, ages ten and twelve. John recently found out that Debbie has been having an affair with his best friend for the last two years, and he is devastated. He is full of anger and finds it almost impossible to control his rage. Debbie realizes that this was not the best way to deal with the growing disconnect that she has felt from him over the years and wishes that they could use this crisis in their marriage as a wake-up call to fix it. John, however, feels strongly that he will never be able to forgive her or trust her again and that their only option is to get a divorce. Once he made this decision, he felt that he needed to tell the children about what happened. One Saturday morning when Debbie was at yoga, John sat down with the kids and told them that their mother had been cheating on him with his best friend and that it was her fault that they were getting divorced. They were obviously devastated and enraged with their mom for causing these problems. They had many questions about what the future would look like for them such as where they would live and how much time would they spend with each parent. John really had no answers for them since none of this had been discussed or agreed upon with Debbie. When she returned home from yoga, she was met by two angry children who were blaming her for being a horrible mother and for destroying their family (and this anger lasted for years). It took eight months for John and Debbie to work out all of the details of their divorce and for Debbie to finally move out into her own place.

During this time, the children lived in fearful limbo, constantly worrying about when and how their life was going to change. They witnessed their parents' almost constant conflict and struggled to get through every day.

TIMING

The first thing to consider is when exactly is the right time to inform the children that you are planning to get divorced. It is problematic both to tell the children too soon (as John did with his children in the previous scenario) as well as to tell them too late. Let me explain why. Once you and your spouse make the decision to divorce, there is usually a lengthy period of time during which you will be going through the process of negotiating or litigating the details of your divorce. During this time, both spouses typically remain in the marital home since one parent moving out is usually based upon all of the financial and legal issues being resolved. Therefore, telling the children early on about the upcoming divorce will result in them living in a state of limbo for many months, anxiously awaiting the next step. Given that none of the details pertaining to custody or parenting schedules have been established, there is virtually no information to give to them regarding what that next step will even look like. The uncertainty can be overwhelming for them. For all of these reasons, it is best not to prematurely open the conversation about the impending divorce with your children. Rather, your goal during this period should be to shield them from any marital conflict, never share any information about the legal proceedings with them, maintain as much consistency and predictability in their lives as possible, and take care of yourself so that your current emotional challenges do not spill over into your relationship with them.

Telling the children about the divorce just prior to one parent moving out is equally problematic. It does not give them ample time to accept the reality that the divorce is actually happening and to process their myriad feelings with you. They need adequate time to wrap their heads around this new reality before it is actually thrust upon them.

Given the need to avoid telling them too early or too late, the optimum time frame to have this conversation is three to four weeks prior to one or both parents moving out of the family home. This seems to be the perfect balance of giving the children enough time to start processing the reality of the divorce, giving you enough time to have developed the specific details about future custody arrangements, and not keeping them in limbo for too long a period of time as they wait for the changes to occur. I often suggest having this conversation on a Friday night or at the start of a vacation week so that the children have a few days at home with you to deal with their feelings before having to return to school.

There may be situations where the two of you may decide to physically and/or emotionally separate while still living together in the same house as you work toward divorce. This may entail sleeping in separate bedrooms, no longer eating meals together, spending minimal time together as a family, and engaging in only minimal communication with each other. With younger children, you may be able to offer them believable explanations for these changes that they will accept (mommy snores so loud that I can't sleep in the same bed as her, daddy is working long hours which is why he is gone so often). However, older children may require a more open explanation, and this then becomes the time to have the detailed conversation with them about the impending divorce.

WHAT SHOULD I SAY?
NO, WHAT SHOULD WE SAY?

This may be one of the most important and difficult conversations that you ever have with your children. It is going to lay the foundation for how they cope with the divorce for years to come and how they process it in their own mind. It is very important to get this right the first time because trying to repair the damage from initial missteps will be very difficult to do, though it is possible.

Let me detail the essential parameters for a healthy, effective conversation about the upcoming divorce with your children.

Do It as a Team

You and your spouse must, if at all possible, have this conversation together with your children. It is crucial for them to see that you can and will continue to work together as their parents, on their behalf, despite the fact that you are getting divorced. You must strive to do this as a focused team, not as adversaries, whose only priority is the well-being of your children.

No Accusations of Blame

There need to be no accusations of blame of either parent, either overtly or subtly, for causing the divorce. Children need to be told that it is a joint decision and that it is no one's fault (even if one or both of you feel strongly that it is). They need to understand that you no longer love each other in the way that a husband and wife should, but that it in no way changes how much you love them. (While I understand the pain and betrayal that led John to tell his children that Debbie's infidelity was to blame for their divorce, the damage that it caused was significant and long-lasting.) This is not the time or the place to prove to your children that you have been wronged or that one of their parents is a despicable human being causing the break-up of the family. Actually, there is never a time or place for that to happen. Rather, the goal of this discussion is to share the sad reality that the marriage is over and to reassure the children that they will never stop being loved and cared for by both of their parents.

Explain at an Age-Appropriate Level

Children should be given explanations that are at a cognitive level appropriate to their age so that they can clearly under-stand what they are being told. This may require talking to children of different ages separately. For example, if you have a four-year-old and a ten-year-old, it may make sense to speak to them individually since they will have very different levels of understanding of what you are trying to explain to them.

Provide Details of the Visitation Plan

It is important to share the details of the parenting time schedule with the children so that they understand exactly when they will be with each parent. Having clear expectations of what their future will look like will help them deal with the fear and uncertainty that the divorce process can cause.

Establish Appropriate Boundaries

Children should not be told about legal or financial issues during this conversation or at any time in the future. You need to explicitly tell them that "this is the adult business of the divorce" and that it is not something that they need to be concerned about or that you will be sharing with them. You do need to reassure them that they will continue to be taken care of by both parents and that their needs will continue to be met as they have been in the past.

Reinforce That Children Are Not the Cause

Children often blame themselves for causing the divorce. This is most typical with younger preschool-age children and in families where there has been a lot of parental conflict around child-rearing issues. Whatever their age, it is very important to clearly and explicitly tell your children that they are in no way responsible for the divorce. You need to reassure them that no one, including them, is to blame or caused this to happen.

Listen, Support, and Comfort

You will not be able to predict how your children will respond to this discussion, regardless of how accurately you think that you can. Your "sensitive child" may appear totally unfazed or your easy-going child may be overwhelmed with sadness and tears. Sometimes children have no immediate reaction at all. The important thing is to give each child the permission to feel whatever they need to feel. Your most important job is to be there to listen, support, and comfort them in whatever ways they appear to need. If they want to talk, listen. If they need to cry, hold them. If they need space to process this on their own, respect that and give it to them. This is not going to be a one-time conversation, but rather one that will continue to take place for days, weeks, and perhaps years to come. Your role is to be available when they come to you with questions and answer them as clearly and age-appropriately as possible. Children will continue to process the divorce throughout their childhood and beyond, and their level of maturity and cognitive development will determine the way in which they are currently thinking about it and the questions that they will ask you. Let them know that you will always be available when they have a need to talk and remind them of this frequently in the days and weeks to come. After that, it will be important to continue checking in with them periodically to assess how they are coping and provide them with the support that they might be needing at the time.

Model Healthy Emotions

It is okay for you to be sad and tearful during this conversation and to share with your children that this is a very painful process for you as well. This actually serves to model for them that it is okay to cry and to express painful emotions. However, it is not appropriate for you to be uncontrollably sobbing and breaking down in a way that will appear scary to them. You do not want to give them the message that they are going to have to take care of you, but rather that you are sad, that it is okay to be sad, and that you are able to be there to take care of them as they deal with their painful feelings. You also need to be cautious about sharing your anger toward your spouse with them. There is no good reason to do this and it will only serve to unnecessarily hurt your children.

CREATING A POSITIVE FOUNDATION

Following these suggestions will not make this conversation any easier but will serve to make it as healthy and productive as possible. It will lay a positive foundation for your family to cope with the next steps in the divorce journey as you work to create a new type of family unit. It is absolutely possible to do this well, to put your children's needs above your own anger and hurt, and to help them best handle this difficult transition in their lives.

I can imagine that the prospect of handling these conversations with grace and composure might feel virtually impossible given the incredible stress, sadness, anger, and pain that you are probably feeling at this time. In the following chapters, I will offer some guidelines and suggestions about how to most effectively deal with these painful emotions and how to get yourself into the right emotional state to best get through the difficult steps along your divorce journey.

6

HOW CHILDREN
OF DIFFERENT AGES
COPE WITH DIVORCE

The age of your child will be a significant determining factor in how they react to and cope with the parental divorce. Understanding the typical age-related reactions will help you to best understand your child's emotional responses and to guide you in how to best support them in dealing with those emotions.

INFANTS AND TODDLERS
(up to age three)

Children of this age are totally dependent upon their parents for their emotional needs and basic care. They look for and respond to consistency in their lives which a divorce can unsettle. They also react emotionally to their parents' affect. Therefore, the three central causes of psychological distress for children of this age are unpredictable daily routines, hostility between parents, and emotional distress of one parent (especially the primary caretaker). This distress in very young children may manifest in regression or backsliding in major developmental tasks such as:

- **Eating**: Your child might start refusing foods that they previously liked or return to using a bottle
- **Emotional regulation**: Your child might start crying more or become more easily frustrated
- **Independence**: Your child may become clingier or more anxious with a caregiver
- **Language**: Your child may revert to previous baby talk
- **Sleeping**: Your child may have increased struggles at bedtime or start having nightmares
- **Toilet training**: Your child may start bedwetting if they were previously dry through the night

Based upon this developmental understanding, children of this age need several specific things to help them cope with parental divorce. These include:

- Consistent and predictable daily schedule of where the child will be and who will be caring for them
- Reduced hostility between parents, especially in front of the child
- Maintenance of affectionate loving care

- Continued regular contact with both parents
- Decreased stress in the caretakers, especially the primary custodial parent if there is one

PRESCHOOL CHILDREN
(ages three to five)

Children of this age are starting to become more advanced cognitively so they can be more confused by the divorce experience than younger children. They tend to have what's referred to as "cognitive egocentrism" which means that they interpret the world in terms of themselves. As a result, they often believe that they caused the divorce and engage in a lot of self-blame (i.e., I was bad, I didn't listen, I fought too much with my sister). Short-term reactions to the divorce tend to be anxiety-based and are often rooted in fear of abandonment. Life becomes full of scary questions such as: What is going to happen to me? Who is going to take care of me? What if they stop loving me? Children can develop regressive behaviors at this age as well, including an increase in separation anxiety, crying at bedtime, bedwetting, whining, tantrums, aggressive behavior, and loss of previously established self-care skills.

To best cope with parental divorce, children at this age are most in need of:

- Careful explanation about parents getting divorced following all of the suggestions detailed in the previous chapter, with special attention to the fact that they are not to blame

- Consistency in day-to-day structure, routines, and rituals within and between both parents' households
- Minimal parental conflict, particularly in front of the child
- Regular and frequent positive contact with both parents
- Extra help and reassurance around separations and transitions which may be very stressful for them

ELEMENTARY AGE
(ages six to eight)

Children at this age are starting to be able to think more abstractly. They have developed a sense of family and an identifiable love for their parents that they are only now beginning to be able to fully appreciate. Therefore, the biggest challenge for these children is dealing with the overwhelming sadness and grief about the loss of the family unit. They can be intensely aware of this sadness and find it difficult to find relief. They can develop frightening fantasies about being abandoned and being left totally alone. In addition, they can hold onto fantasies of reconciliation for long periods of time wishing their parents will get back together and struggling to accept the finality of the divorce. They can rely on wishful thinking to cope with the pain of loss, so parents of children this age need to be careful not to do things that might feed the child's hope of them becoming a family again (like spending too much time together as a family post-divorce). Children can also start developing loyalty conflicts at this age. If there are parental pressures for them to take sides, children try to be loyal to both parents, frequently resulting in considerable psychological distress.

In order to best cope, children at this age need the following:

- Frequent reassurance about the consistency of regular, predictable parenting time
- Empathy/support by the parents for their painful feelings
- Normalizing their feelings ("it is absolutely normal and understandable that you feel this way")
- Not to be involved in adult concerns (such as money, legal issues) since it only serves to fuel their anxiety
- Not to be brought into parental conflict or put in the position of having to choose between parents (one of the greatest post-divorce gifts you can give to your child is the explicit/direct permission to have a positive relationship with the other parent)
- Structured special time with each parent to assure them of both parents' continued love and availability (be sure that some of this time is devoted to play and other fun activities)

LATER ELEMENTARY AGE
(ages nine to twelve)

As children get older, they are more cognitively able to develop a realistic understanding of the divorce process. They are also developing a more sophisticated sense of interpersonal relationships which can give rise to strong feelings of divided loyalties. Taking sides and aligning with one parent can become a significant problem for children of this age, especially when one parent is actively disparaging or bad-mouthing the other. The predominant emotion seen in children of this age tends to be anger, and it can often be intense. Somatic/physical complaints, such as headaches and stomachaches, are also common and may be linked to periods of heightened stress. Children at this age often get drafted into parentified roles ("now that your dad is gone, you are the man of the house") which can also be very stressful for them. Given that children this age are more involved with peers, school, and sports, they may attempt to cope with the divorce by distancing themselves from the family through spending increasing amounts of time engaging in these activities. This is positive coping and should be encouraged.

Children of this age are most in need of:

- Open discussion about the divorce
- Not being put in the middle of parental conflicts
- Not being placed in the role of co-parent/confidante
- Understanding about the underlying dynamics of their anger and not having their anger met by your anger
- Encouragement of their involvement in outside activities while still valuing family time

ADOLESCENTS
(ages thirteen to eighteen)

This is a time of substantial flux on all developmental fronts, and all adolescents need a lot of emotional support, love, and firm guidance to confront these considerable age-related challenges. With divorce, they now need to face the difficult task of adjusting to two sets of significant changes: those that normally arise for teenagers and those specifically related to the divorce process. The stakes are also higher at this age given that they are now capable of expressing feelings of distress in alarming ways (such as drug use, sexual promiscuity, and legal troubles).

Adolescents are often shocked to learn of divorce since they have learned to accept parental conflict as a way of life. Surprise can quickly turn to anger. While the younger child may try to get their parents back together; the adolescent may try to get back at their parents. They may begin viewing their parents in extremely negative terms due to their disappointment in them, which is in direct conflict with their love and need for them. They are developing a higher level of right and wrong, so one parent often gets condemned as the cause of the divorce. They are especially vulnerable to parental conflicts and are often forced to choose in custody disputes. As a result, loyalty conflicts are very common at this age. Many teenagers are also forced into adult roles. For some, this results in greater maturity, and for others, it results in the complete opposite. It is important that they be given both time and permission to live their own lives apart from family responsibilities. Finally, issues of sexuality are central at this time and experiencing parents' overt sexuality (finding out that a parent has been having an affair, dealing with parental dating) can be very stressful.

Given these particular developmental challenges, adolescents going through divorce are in need of:

- Open discussion of their age-related struggles and divorce-related issues
- Not being exposed to parental conflict
- Not being put in parental/adult roles and having adequate time not to be responsible and just to be a teenager
- Opportunities, either in the home or with a professional, to talk about their wide range of emotions
- Structure and consistency in their lives including predictable limit-setting and guidance (distressed parents can become lax or overly permissive out of guilt or stress and this can result in anxiety or feelings of not being cared about)

As can be seen from this discussion, children of different ages have some very age-specific reactions and needs as well as some which transcend age and occur throughout childhood. The more you are familiar with these differences, the more you will be able to help your child of a particular age cope with the challenges of the divorce. This understanding will help you best anticipate and respond to your children's needs so that you can most effectively help them cope with their divorce journey in the healthiest possible way.

ADULT CHILDREN

It is important to understand that parental divorce can be very difficult for adult children as well. While parents are often very concerned about the emotional toll that their divorce will have on their young children, it is a fairly common misconception that it will not be that emotionally challenging for their grown children. While it will clearly affect them differently, it will inevitably have a major emotional impact on them and, as with younger children, there are steps that can be taken to minimize this negative toll.

Parents of adult children of divorce often turn to their children for both emotional and financial support. Boundaries often get blurred and details regarding very personal marital/divorce issues get inappropriately discussed with adult children. Parents can attempt to get their children to side with them and see things only from their one perspective. They can put their children in the position of having to choose one parent over the other, both in terms of time spent and perceived loyalty. Family traditions, particularly related to holidays, will typically change drastically which will present an additional loss for the adult child (as will the potential sale of the family home). The divorcing parent may also be financially challenged and turn to their child for monetary support, potentially creating a tremendous amount of stress for the child and their family.

Given these challenges, adult children of divorce are in need of:

- Not being asked to choose between parents
- Not being put in the role of therapist or primary emotional support
- Understanding and empathy regarding the emotional impact that the divorce is going to have on them
- Maintaining appropriate boundaries between parental issues and "children's" issues

7

HOW TO TAKE CARE OF YOURSELF AS YOU GO THROUGH THE DIVORCE JOURNEY

As I'm sure you are well aware, the period before, during, and after a divorce can be extremely stressful. While it is important for all of us to have a variety of coping strategies available to us throughout the course of our lives, these strategies become even more essential when we are going through periods of intense stress such as a divorce. You need to engage in effective self-care not only for yourself, but so that you can also be there to best support your children as they try to cope with all of the changes in their lives. It is very easy to push these things aside as other more pressing things seem to take priority. However, prioritizing self-care is imperative and will maximize your chances of getting through this stressful time as healthy and emotionally intact as possible.

COPING STRATEGIES

The following is a list of coping strategies that you can utilize to take care of yourself now and at any time in the future when you might need them again. Please try all of them, see which seem to work best for you, and then work to build the most effective ones into your daily routine.

Use Your Support System

It is important to develop and utilize your support systems (i.e., family, friends, clergy, support groups, divorce coach) now more than ever. It is essential for you to have people to talk to about what you are going through. Work to accept that you are not being a burden when you turn to these important people in your life when you need them the most. You would clearly do the same for them, and probably already have. Also, do not allow yourself to believe that divorce is a shameful secret that you need to keep to yourself. It is a significant life event like any other and which you have every right to talk about with the significant people in your life. Let your friends and family be there for you. Do not push them away when you need them the most.

Give Yourself Permission to Grieve

It is important to acknowledge that you are grieving for the loss of your family as you knew it and to let yourself fully grieve. Pushing away the pain is never an effective strategy since it only serves to prolong the process of resolving your grief.

Stages of Grief

Some further thoughts on grieving: As you may already know, there are stages of grief that people typically go through when dealing with a painful loss. Divorce clearly involves a tremendous amount of loss, even if you are the one who has initiated it. While not everyone goes through all of the stages or goes through them in particular order, they are a roadmap for understanding the types of feelings that you may experience as you make your way through the grieving process. These stages include:

1) **Denial**. This initial stage helps you to cope with the shock of the loss by not being overly flooded by intense emotion. This coping mechanism helps you pace your feelings of grief by only letting in as much as you can handle at the time.

2) **Anger**. This is a necessary part of the healing process, and it is important to let yourself feel your anger. However, it is crucial that you express this anger appropriately (by talking to trusted people, journaling, or through physical activity) and that it does not come out physically or abusively toward the people close to you. There are typically many feelings underlying this anger, and you will go through the process of exploring those feelings as the grieving process continues.

3) **Bargaining**. You may wish that life could return to what it was and that you could go back in time and

fix your mistakes. You may find fault in yourself and focus on what you could have done differently. Accept this as a normal part of the grieving process rather than as confirmation that you are to blame for everything bad that is happening in your life at this time.

4) **Depression**. Your attention may now start to focus on the present and your grief and sadness may intensify. It may feel to you like this feeling will last forever, but you need to frequently remind yourself that it will not. Rather, it is a normal part of the grieving process and one which you will need to navigate your way through in order to get to the point of acceptance.

5) **Acceptance**. This is the point that you begin to acknowledge that your new marital status is your present reality. You learn to live with the fact that you are now divorced and that this is your new normal. It doesn't imply that you are happy about it, only that you accept that your life is forever changed and that you must re-adjust and find new ways to be happy.

Let Go of Self Blame

You need to work to let go of the sense of shame and failure that you might be feeling. Divorce is not a shameful event or one that suggests that you are a personal failure. Rather, it is an all too common life transition that typically both of you played a part in and for which you share joint responsibility.

It is important to stop "beating yourself up" for your marriage ending and to strive to let go of the self-blame and guilt that you might be feeling.

Avoid Substance Abuse

It is essential that you avoid the excessive use of alcohol or drugs as a means of self-medicating your painful feelings. This is never an effective solution and generally only serves to create a whole new set of problems with which you and your children will need to cope. For example, most substances lessen control over your feelings, resulting in an increased chance of over-reacting, acting out, or in some other way exacerbating an already difficult situation. If your symptoms of anxiety or depression are unmanageable, seek professional therapeutic help and explore the utility of a prescribed medication trial in order to help you get through this difficult time.

Express Your Feelings

Start keeping a journal as a means of expressing some of the challenging thoughts/feelings that this process elicits. This can be a very helpful way of getting things "out of your head" so that they are not just a source of endless rumination.

Maintain Self Care

This is the time to develop and/or maintain a healthy lifestyle. This includes eating well, getting an adequate amount of sleep, exercising regularly, and consistently utilizing stress management strategies such as yoga, meditation, and massage.

Maintain Healthy Sleep Habits

It is very common for stress to negatively impact your sleep. There are a number of changes that you can make in order to improve your sleep health. These include:

- Try going to bed at the same time each night and waking up at the same time each morning, including on the weekends

- Establish a nightly bedtime routine that is consistent and promotes relaxation

- Make sure your bedroom is dark, quiet, relaxing, and at a comfortable sleeping temperature

- Dedicate your bed to sleep and sex (maybe not now but hopefully in the future) and nothing else

- Remove electronic devices such as TVs, computers, and smartphones from the bedroom and limit screen time before going to sleep

- Avoid large meals, caffeine, and alcohol before bedtime

- Limit daytime naps

- Exercise regularly, preferably around the same time each day, since being physically active during the day can help you fall asleep more easily at night

- Develop some relaxation strategies to utilize when you are having trouble turning your mind off at bedtime (focusing on your breathing, imagining yourself in some beautiful/peaceful place, progressive muscle relaxation)

- If you are lying awake for an extended period of time it is best to get up for a while, do something quiet and relaxing for twenty to thirty minutes, and then return to bed and try to fall asleep again (you don't want your mind to associate your bed with the frustration that can develop with sleep problems)

All of these stress management strategies are readily available to you and offer you powerful tools to help you cope with your heightened level of stress. But they are only as good as your willingness to try them. It is unfortunately very common when people are feeling overwhelmed for them to put taking care of themselves as the lowest of their priorities. This is not the time to do that. It is the time to put taking care of yourself at the top of your list and to build it into your day on a regular basis. You will be better for it, as will your children.

8

SUPPORTING YOUR CHILDREN AS THEY GO THROUGH THE DIVORCE JOURNEY

Most of the stress management strategies described in the last chapter will also be effective coping mechanisms for your children. Remember that you are a powerful role model for them, so seeing you employing these self-care strategies will be a motivator for them to do so as well. In fact, doing these things together can be a fun bonding experience and a way of motivating all of you to take care of yourselves during this stressful time.

There are some additional things that are within your power to do to help your children cope with the divorce process. These include:

TALK AND LISTEN REGULARLY

It is essential that you create frequent opportunities for your children to talk openly with you about their feelings. Since they may not be comfortable initiating these conversations, it will be important for you to do so. Start by asking open-ended questions (ones that don't require a simple yes or no answer) such as:

- How have you been feeling since we talked to you about the divorce?
- What are some of your greatest fears about how things will be in your life now?
- How can I best support you as we go through this process? What do you need from me now?

It is also extremely important for you to be a good listener. You need to work to really hear and understand what your child is saying to you. Try to paraphrase and reflect back what you think you heard ("it sounds like you are feeling really scared that you won't ever see your dad again") to be sure that you got it right. A parent's natural tendency is to want to solve their children's problems and eliminate their pain, but it is unrealistic to assume that you have the power to do this for them. What your child needs most now, and what you are realistically able to provide, is simply for you to understand their feelings and to know that you will always be there to help them cope with those feelings as they develop. Listen, support, and comfort them in their pain.

MINIMIZE PARENTAL CONFLICT

The greatest predictor of how your children will cope with divorce is the level of parental conflict that they are exposed to. Given that fact, one of the most powerful ways that you can help them now and in the future is to minimize the amount of conflict that they witness between you and their other parent. Your top priorities need to be never fighting in front of them, never putting them in the middle of your conflicts, not using them as pawns in your battles, not making them choose between the two of you, and not asking them to be a messenger or go-between. Your commitment to this will be another one of the powerful gifts that you can give your children as you all navigate through the divorce process. I will discuss all of this in greater detail in Chapter 11 on how to most effectively co-parent.

MAINTAIN ROUTINES

Your children will need as much consistency, predictability, and structure in their lives as it is possible for you to provide. Given that so much is already changing, it is essential to maintain those things that do not absolutely need to change. For example, now would not be the best time to switch day care providers or find a new ballet school. It is also important to maintain the structure that your children have been accustomed to, even if at times you feel too overwhelmed or exhausted to make that happen. Bedtime should remain the same, children should continue sleeping in their own beds (rather than with you), homework needs to be done and checked regularly, and limits on screen time need to be followed. This structure and consistency will help your children understand that not everything is changing and that you are still available to them as their loving parent despite the emotional challenges that you are facing in your life.

MAINTAIN BOUNDARIES

It is very important that you maintain appropriate boundaries with your children, especially with the older ones. You need to remember that they are not your friend, your confidante, or your therapist. You need to not burden them with your emotional issues. You should never talk to them about legal proceedings or financial problems. You need to let them continue to be children, free from the adult business that their parents are tasked with handling.

ASSESS FUNCTIONING

You need to be a sensitive observer of how your children are coping during this difficult time. It is important to strike a balance between expecting some changes in mood and behavior as normal and not ignoring significant signs that they are struggling and need help (as detailed in Chapter 9, entitled Warning Signs of Trouble Coping).

It is so important to remember that children can get through this process with minimal emotional damage if you follow the suggestions made in this and in subsequent chapters. It is not inevitable that they are emotionally destroyed by your divorce. Yes, the process will be stressful, but you have the power to minimize their stress as well as to help them develop strategies to best cope with it.

9

WARNING SIGNS OF TROUBLE COPING: SYMPTOMS OF STRESS IN CHILDREN AND ADULTS

Going through a divorce is an extremely stressful life event, and it will inevitably take an emotional toll on both the children and the adults involved. It is important to be able to tell the difference between a typical acute stress reaction (which is characterized by a sudden onset and a brief course) versus one that becomes more long-term and problematic over time. In doing so, you will be more aware of the warning signs of severe emotional distress and be more knowledgeable about when to seek professional help for either you or your child should it become necessary.

STRESS REACTIONS IN CHILDREN

Case 1

Rachel is nine years old. She found out several months ago that her parents are getting divorced. She initially seemed to be handling things pretty well until she started waking up in the middle of the night with bad dreams. These lasted for a couple of months and then seemed to go away on their own. Once her dad actually moved out, she started to develop a number of other anxiety-based symptoms. She frequently complained of stomachaches in the morning and tried desperately to stay home from school. Several times a week she wound up in the school nurse's office complaining of not feeling well and wanting to go home. The transitions from her mom's house to her dad's became extremely stressful and emotional. She would cry inconsolably when she left her mom and would become angry and defiant when she was with her dad. Her parents gave her lots of opportunities to talk about her painful feelings and continued to reinforce that they will always love her and always be there to help and support her. After a few months, these symptoms started to slowly improve, and Rachel eventually returned to be the happy child that she was before she learned of her parent's impending divorce.

Children tend to display psychological distress in different ways than adults. Given that they often lack the ability to identify and verbalize painful feelings, there is a greater tendency for those feelings to be acted out behaviorally. This could start immediately after learning about the divorce or after one parent actually moves out of the home. For example, your young child might start having tantrums after transitioning from one home to another or regress in their toilet training. Your previously well-behaved and compliant school-aged child may start acting out. This can take many forms including testing limits, breaking rules, fighting more with siblings. You may start getting more frequent calls from school reporting an increase in defiance or behaviors that result in detention. Separations from you may become more difficult and they may start refusing to go to school. Your teenager may start looking for any opportunity to instigate an argument with you and may be caught drinking for the first time or missing a curfew.

In addition to these behavioral changes, you may also notice a change in your child's mood during and after a divorce. Anxiety and depression tend to be the most typical symptoms and can present themselves in a variety of ways. Children can become extremely scared at bedtime and wake up frequently during the night with bad dreams. They may start complaining of headaches or stomach aches and spend an increasing amount of time in the school nurse's office due to those complaints. They may be scared to go to school for fear of getting sick there or because they are worried that something tragic will happen to you while you are not together. Your previously happy child may also simply look sad, which may be a reflection of the grief that they are experiencing. Remember that they are going through the same stages of grief as you are.

It is important to note that all of these are normal responses to stress in children and should initially not be a cause for alarm. Rather, they should be an indication that your child is struggling to cope with the divorce, and that they are in need of opportunities to talk about their feelings with you on a regular basis. You need to provide them with reassurance that they will continue to be loved and nurtured by both parents, despite the end of your marriage. You need to continue to be a consistent parent and follow through on your previously established rules and consequences for breaking those rules. This is NOT the time to become overly permissive out of guilt for causing them this distress. The best way for you to show them that you will always love and protect them is for you to maintain the rules and expectations that have always been a part of their life. Consistency and predictability are what your children need most during this tumultuous time, and it is your job to provide that for them to the best of your ability.

Parents frequently ask whether seeking professional help for your child at this time of acute stress is necessary. My typical response is that it may not be absolutely necessary, but that it could certainly be helpful. Sometimes, children do not want to burden a struggling parent with their problems, so they keep their feelings to themselves. It also might not feel safe to tell a parent how angry they feel for their lives being turned upside down. Developing a therapeutic relationship with a mental health professional at this time will provide your child with an outlet for all of their painful feelings, help them learn a variety of strategies to more effectively cope with their stress, and hopefully prevent these normal stress-related symptoms from developing into something more chronic and problematic.

It is also very important for you to inform school personnel of the stressful situation occurring within your family at this time. This could help them understand any changes in your child's behavior or mood that they observe within the school setting and put those changes into the proper context. The school counselor or social worker can be an additional source of support for helping your child cope during this difficult time. They often run a support group at school for children whose parents are divorcing (in my area it is called "Banana Splits"). It provides children with the opportunity to connect with peers who are going through the same thing and who can empathize with what they are experiencing.

There are various indications that a normal stress reaction has turned into a more serious mental health issue, and it is important that you be able to recognize these symptoms in your child should they develop.

Warning Signs in Children

- Any talk about self-harm ("I wish I was dead"; "my life is so horrible I wish it was over")
- Any acts of self-harm (i.e., cutting, substance abuse, intentional drug overdose)
- Changes in appetite resulting in significant weight loss or gain
- Lack of desire to engage in usual social, athletic, or school activities
- Prolonged difficulty sleeping
- Significant change in school performance
- Prolonged periods of sadness, anxiety, or anger
- Refusal to spend time with one or both parents
- Any of the above behavior/mood changes that last for an extended period of time (i.e., several months after establishing a "new normal" in your lives)

If your child starts manifesting any of these symptoms, and if you have not already engaged the help of a mental health professional, now is the time to do so. Your child may be exhibiting signs of clinical depression or an anxiety disorder and they are in need of therapeutic intervention to help them manage and resolve these symptoms. If they are verbalizing suicidal thoughts or engaging in self-harmful behavior you must immediately take them to your nearest emergency room where they can quickly be evaluated, and steps can be taken to maintain their safety.

STRESS REACTIONS IN ADULTS

Case 2

Karen is a forty-six-year-old woman who is in the process of divorcing her husband of twenty-two years. Despite the fact that she was the one who initiated the divorce, she is struggling to cope with all of the feelings that it has elicited. She frequently lays awake for hours unable to sleep, obsessing about all of the ways in which her life is going to change. She is terrified about her ability to support herself and her two children, despite knowing that her husband will be required to pay child support. She worries that she will never be in another relationship and that she will be destined to be alone and lonely for the rest of her life. She has also started to worry about her health given the weird physical symptoms that she has been experiencing over the past few months. She often feels nauseous, alternates between having diarrhea or being constipated, and is constantly tired. Her thoughts often get stuck on the possibility that she has stomach cancer and that she is going to die and leave her children motherless. She decided it was time to see her primary care doctor who cautiously sent her for a battery of tests, all of which came out normal. Her doctor concluded that her symptoms were all related to stress given what was currently going on in her life. She was referred to a therapist whom she started seeing on a regular basis. After several months of treatment, these symptoms started to slowly subside.

Stress can manifest in adults in many different ways as well. These reactions tend to fall into two major categories: physical and emotional. Given the very strong mind-body connection, it is very common for adults under stress to experience a variety of somatic symptoms. These can include tension/migraine headaches, gastric distress (irritable bowel, heartburn, nausea), chronic muscle tension, jaw pain (from teeth clenching/ grinding), chest pain, rapid heartbeat, hypertension, skin rashes, and low energy/fatigue. Common emotional manifestations of stress include anxiety, panic attacks, sleep disturbance, compulsive over-eating or loss of appetite, irritability, anger, frequent crying, feeling overwhelmed, sadness, mood swings, difficulty concentrating, racing thoughts, and difficulty making decisions. Adults can also exhibit behavioral changes in response to stress, but not to the extent that is typically seen in children. These behavioral changes can include increased smoking/substance abuse, excessive gambling, impulse buying, reduced work efficiency, or paying less attention to appearance.

As with children, seeking professional help in the presence of these stress-related symptoms can be extremely beneficial and could prevent the development of more serious mental health or medical issues. The goal of therapy at this time will be to learn more effective strategies to cope with the stress, loss, and grief that is negatively impacting your life.

It is also important for you to be able to recognize the potential symptoms that are suggestive of the development of a more serious mental health problem. While some of these symptoms may be part of a normal stress reaction, it is when they persist on a more chronic basis or become more severe and interfere with functioning that they become a greater cause for concern. If you have a prior history or mental illness or there is a history of mental illness within your family, there is a greater chance that your current symptoms may be the intensifying of an underlying mental illness triggered by your heightened level of stress.

Warning Signs in Adults

Changes in your mood or behavior that should be of concern include:

- Persistent sleep disturbance (i.e., trouble falling asleep, frequent waking, difficulty getting up in the morning)
- Appetite disturbance resulting in significant weight loss or gain
- Loss of interest in previously enjoyed activities
- Hopelessness about the future ever getting better
- Suicidal thoughts or behavior
- Frequent fatigue
- Lack of motivation or drive
- Panic attacks that become more frequent or intense
- Social isolation and withdrawal from people
- Intense irritability or anger
- Severe mood swings
- Inability to function at home or at work

If you recognize any of these symptoms in yourself it is crucial that you seek professional help in the form of therapy, medication, or both. It is not a sign of weakness to need or to seek help. You are human, you are going through a very difficult time, and sometimes we are not able to cope with these problems on our own. You owe it to yourself and to your children to pursue the necessary help so that you are able to best support them and yourself as you go through this difficult time in your life. The next chapter will guide you through the process of finding an appropriate therapist to help you manage all of these emotional responses.

10

HOW TO FIND
A THERAPIST

The first step before you begin the process of searching for a therapist is admitting to yourself that you are in need of one. People often feel like it is a sign of weakness or failure to admit that they need professional help. In fact, it is quite the opposite. Acknowledging the need for help is a brave and powerful decision that reflects your commitment to yourself and to your family. It is not shameful to need help, it is simply human.

Once you have decided that you are in need of a good therapist, finding one can be a challenging task. People frequently don't have a clue about where to even begin. Asking yourself a few basic questions may help you get started:

1) What are the issues that I want to deal with in therapy?

2) Does it matter to me whether I work with a male or a female therapist?

3) Does the particular credential of the therapist matter to me?

4) Does the therapist have to be a participating provider with my insurance company?

5) Am I looking for a therapist with a specific theoretical orientation or style?

6) Once I have answered these questions, how do I actually go about finding a therapist that meets my criteria?

WHAT ARE THE ISSUES THAT I WANT TO DEAL WITH IN THERAPY?

Clarifying why you are pursuing therapy can be very helpful in determining the kind of therapist that will best meet your needs. For example, there is a big difference between a therapist who primarily provides support and guidance in dealing with life stressors versus one who can diagnose and treat a serious mental illness. Therefore, you need to have some clarity about your goals for therapy in order to find a therapist who can best help you meet those goals. You also need to identify particular problem areas that you want to focus on since many therapists have specific areas of expertise such as divorce, substance abuse, eating disorders, trauma, working with children, or LGBTQ issues.

DOES IT MATTER TO ME WHETHER I WORK WITH A MALE OR A FEMALE THERAPIST?

The choice of whether you prefer to work with a male or female therapist is a highly personal one. For some people it is a totally irrelevant factor whereas for others it is extremely important to work with a therapist of a particular gender. Deciding for yourself before starting to look for a provider will help to focus your search from the outset.

DOES THE PARTICULAR CREDENTIAL OF THE THERAPIST MATTER TO ME?

You also need to determine whether you want to work with a psychologist, social worker, licensed mental health counselor, or with someone who has no academic credential. (Bias alert: I am a psychologist and strongly believe that we are the best-trained mental health professionals.) If you require medication in addition to therapy, your choices are to work either with a psychiatrist, psychiatric nurse practitioner, or your primary care doctor. The differences between these various mental health professionals are:

Psychologist

A psychologist with a clinical practice has completed either a PhD or PsyD in Clinical or Counseling Psychology. They are extensively trained in all aspects of the diagnosis and treatment of psychiatric illness. They focus on providing psychotherapy to people who present with a broad range of problems such as depression, anxiety, post-traumatic stress disorder, and other stress reactions. They generally do not prescribe medication other than in certain states and settings where psychologists with advanced training in psychopharmacology have prescription privileges (Iowa, Idaho, Illinois, New Mexico, Louisiana, in the Indian Health Service, and in the military). They are licensed in their state to provide psychological services and are eligible for insurance reimbursement.

Social Worker

A social worker has completed a two-year master's degree in Social Work (MSW). Once they complete two years of supervised professional experience, they are eligible to sit for their state licensure exam and earn the title of Licensed Clinical Social Worker (LCSW). They are trained to help people cope with life-changing events, coordinate community support services, as well as to diagnose and treat mental illness. They are eligible for insurance reimbursement.

Licensed Mental Health Counselor (LMHC)/Licensed Professional Counselor (LPC)

These are two different titles for essentially the same occupation within the mental health field. LMHCs and LPCs have a two-year master's degree and their services are insurance reimbursable once they have one to two years of professional service and pass their state licensing exam. Their focus of treatment is on helping people develop concrete strategies to resolve all types of problems in their life.

Counselor/Therapist/Coach

These are all titles that anyone can use, and which require no specific level of training. There is no licensure requirement that serves to guarantee a basic level of professionalism, competence, or ethical standard. Services provided by these individuals are not insurance reimbursable.

Psychiatrist

A psychiatrist has earned an MD degree after completing medical school plus has extensive advanced training in both diagnosing/treating mental illness and psychopharmacology (medications for psychiatric illness). Their primary role is prescribing medication (i.e., medication management) with only a small percentage of them providing therapy as well. Typically, a patient who requires medication will see both a psychiatrist (every two to three months once they have been stabilized on a particular medication) and a therapist (usually weekly or every other week, especially at the start) since the evidence suggest that this combination is the treatment of choice for individuals with mental illness. Psychiatrists are licensed within their state to practice medicine, and their services are eligible for insurance reimbursement.

Psychiatric Nurse Practitioner (PNP)

These individuals are advanced practice nurses who function in the same way as a psychiatrist, typically under the supervision of a physician. They are licensed within their state and are eligible for insurance reimbursement.

Primary Care Provider (PCP)

PCPs are able to prescribe psychiatric medication, but they vary greatly in their interest and expertise in doing so. My recommendation is that you seek out a psychiatrist or PNP if you are dealing with serious symptoms that are interfering with your ability to function (in the same way that you would want to consult with a specially trained cardiologist if you were experiencing serious heart-related symptoms).

There are many ethical and competent professionals to be found in each of these categories. You need to match your needs with the level of education/training and particular areas of expertise of providers within these various categories of mental health professionals and choose the one that seems best suited to your presenting issues.

DOES THE THERAPIST HAVE TO BE A PARTICIPATING PROVIDER WITH MY INSURANCE COMPANY?

In order for your insurance company to reimburse the therapist for the mental health services that they provide they must be a participating provider for your particular medical insurance company. If they are a provider, your only financial obligation will be to satisfy your yearly deductible and then pay your co-pay (assuming you have one) for each therapy session. If the therapist does not participate with your insurance plan, then you will be responsible for the entire cost of every session unless your policy has an out-of-network benefit which typically reimburses for 80 percent of the cost. While paying out of pocket without the use of insurance can become quite costly, a benefit of doing so is that your records can never be shared with your insurance carrier without your permission which assures a greater level of confidentiality than if your insurance is covering those services. Of course, you always have the choice to not use your insurance and pay out of pocket in order to ensure maximum confidentiality for you or your child.

AM I LOOKING FOR A THERAPIST WITH A SPECIFIC THEORETICAL ORIENTATION OR STYLE?

Every therapist has their own individual personality and style of doing therapy, and it is important to think about the qualities that might best suit your personality and presenting issues. Are you looking for a therapist who is fairly passive and just listens or would you prefer someone who is more active and direct? Do you think you would prefer working with a therapist who is more casual and laid back or one who is serious and formal?

Having some clarity about this will be helpful when you start searching for an appropriate therapist.

Theoretical orientation refers to the underlying beliefs that guide a therapist's practice. For example, a cognitive-behavioral therapist (CBT) believes that the way in which people think about things determines the way they feel about them. Therefore, the goal of therapy is to challenge people's distorted cognitions with the goal of improving their mood and their destructive behavior. In contrast to that approach, a psychoanalytically trained therapist focuses on bringing repressed fears, unconscious impulses, and wounds developed in childhood into the conscious mind as a means of healing current emotional problems. You may not really be sure about what theoretical orientation best suits your needs but asking a potential therapist about their particular belief system might give you some insight into how they might go about treating your particular presenting problems.

It is also useful to ask a potential therapist about the extent of their experience and expertise working with people with similar presenting issues as yours. For example, if you are looking for a therapist to help your child cope with your impending divorce, you would want to ask specifically whether they are trained in doing psychotherapy with children, and how many similar cases they have worked with during the course of their practice.

ONCE I HAVE ANSWERED THESE QUESTIONS, HOW DO I ACTUALLY GO ABOUT FINDING A THERAPIST THAT MEETS MY CRITERIA?

Now that you have answered these questions for yourself, the next step is starting to look for a therapist who fits the criteria that you have established for an appropriate therapist. There are several possible ways of going about this:

- Get potential referrals from trusted friends, colleagues, medical professionals, clergy, attorneys

- Call your insurance company and get a list of participating therapists in your area

- Search online for therapists' websites or reviews

- Contact your local/state/national psychological associations for provider lists

- Contact the National Register of Health Service Psychologists for provider lists

Once you develop a list of potential therapists, spend some time calling their offices and gathering information about their services. See how long it takes to get a return call, either from the therapist or office staff. That will tell you a lot about their availability and responsiveness, which will be important if you decide to work with them. See if you can set up a short call with the therapist to get a feel for their personality and style. Ask about their approach to therapy and specific areas of expertise and see how they match your particular needs.

You will never truly be able to determine a good fit until you have actually had an opportunity to meet the therapist in person. It takes time to establish a trusting therapeutic relationship, but you should quickly have a sense whether you "click" with the person you have chosen. If you don't, keep looking. It is important not to give up on therapy if you do not immediately find that good fit. The therapeutic relationship is a very important part of the treatment, and it may take some time and effort to find a therapist with whom you feel comfortable.

There are many wonderful therapists in your community. Going through the process outlined above will maximize your chances of finding one who will best meet your needs and provide you with a truly meaningful and successful therapeutic experience.

11

HOW TO MOST EFFECTIVELY CO-PARENT

You and your eventual ex-spouse will be connected forever if you have children together. This is a reality that you need to accept and embrace (this is assuming that it is safe for the two of you to continue co-parenting your children and that you have both agreed to play a role in raising them post-divorce). It is imperative that you develop the skills necessary to effectively co-parent your children so as to best meet their needs as they grow into adulthood. Doing so will assure that your children will have the best possible chance of navigating their way through the divorce journey in as healthy a way as possible. Conversely, poor co-parenting can have devastating effects and can cause children serious emotional damage. Therefore, your goal must be to avoid that at all costs. Focus on the positive and doing what is best for your child.

Do Not Let This Be Your Family

Steve and Lisa have been divorced for a year and they have an eight-year-old son Ethan. Their divorce was extremely bitter, and they are both full of anger toward the other. Despite this, they have joint custody of Ethan, so there are many things that they really need to be communicating about with each other. This unfortunately never seems to happen. Lisa recently took Ethan to the pediatrician and was told that he needed to have his tonsils removed but didn't share this with Steve until two days before the surgery. She scheduled it for a day that Steve was going to be out of town for work, so he was not able to be there to support his son. Ethan's transitions between his two homes are full of tension since his parents use that as a time to air their issues with each other. He often runs out of the car and quickly into his room, so he doesn't need to hear them arguing. There is never a day that goes by that he doesn't have to listen to one parent saying mean things about the other. He just wants to scream at them to shut up but usually just quietly sits there until it is over. Sometimes his mom will ask him which home he likes better, hers or his dad's. He wonders how he can possibly answer that question without hurting someone's feelings, so he tries not to answer at all. School events are usually very stressful for him since he never knows which parent he should sit with. Regardless of whom he chooses, one of them is going to be hurt or angry. His dad often asks him to tell his mom about changes in his work schedule. He wonders why his dad can't just tell her himself and wishes he wouldn't put him in this weird position, especially since it usually makes her angry.

Ethan's pain in this scenario is almost palpable. You must do everything within your power to not let this happen to your child! The key to being effective co-parents is for you and your ex-spouse to rise above your own issues with each other, on your children's behalf, and to work together as a team to provide them with the love, guidance, and support that they will need from both of you. You must always remember that their needs are paramount, and this should guide every decision and action that you take pertaining to them.

CO-PARENTING GUIDELINES

What follows are a number of guidelines to follow as you venture into the role of co-parents:

Allow Children to Love Both Parents

Give children permission to love both parents and to enjoy spending time with both of you. Be clear with them that you are not jealous of the time that they spend with the other parent, and that it is important to you that they have a good relationship with both of you.

Keep Children Out of the Middle

Do not put children in the position of having to take sides or choose one of you over the other. This applies to many contexts. For example, don't give them your side of an argument with their other parent and ask them their opinion regarding who they think is right. Do not ask a child to choose which parent they would rather spend their birthday with. Do not ask whose present they liked better or who took them on a better vacation. Do not ask at whose house they have more fun. All of these situations require the child to make a choice of one parent over the other. This is a horrible choice for a child to have to make and one which you should never ask them to make.

Minimize Conflict

You need to avoid arguing in front of your children at all costs. I will remind you that the greatest single predictor of how your children will adapt to the divorce is the level of conflict between the two of you. You will, undoubtedly, have disagreements, but they need to be addressed and resolved when the children are not present. Beyond not fighting in front of the children, it is also vitally important for the two of you to treat each other respectfully and cordially in their presence. Sarcasm, nasty remarks, or simply ignoring one another creates an environment of tension that your children will certainly feel and will start to dread.

Avoid Secrets

Do not ask children to keep secrets from the other parent or to lie to them for you. At the most basic level, this is not behavior that you want to model or to teach them. You also want them to understand that you are a co-parenting team who work together, not against each other. This sort of request is another subtle way of putting them in the position of having to take sides which is something that you need to avoid doing at all times.

Never Bad Mouth the Other Parent

Do not say negative things about the other parent in front of the children. There are few things as painful for a child as hearing someone that they care about and respect saying mean and hurtful things about another person that they equally love, especially if those people are their parents. It is also important to set the same standard for other family members, especially grandparents. They may be struggling with their own divorce-related feelings and consequently may be tempted to share their feelings of anger toward their adult child's ex-spouse.

Respect Boundaries

Do not force children to share details about their time with the other parent. It is fine to ask generally about how a visit went, what they did, and if they had a good time. It is not okay to interrogate your children upon their return home about every detail of the visit, the other parent's behavior, or the behavior of their significant other. Let your children guide the conversation so that they don't feel pressured to provide a detailed account of their visit.

Respect Privacy

Give your child privacy when they are talking to the other parent. If they have a regular nightly phone call or FaceTime/Skype/Zoom, allow them to do this in the privacy of their room without you sitting over their shoulder listening to the conversation (assuming that they aren't so young that they need your help to facilitate this call). This is their relationship with their other parent and giving them this space confirms that you support and trust that relationship and do not feel the need to have to supervise it in any way.

Communicate Directly with the Other Parent

Do not ask your child to be a messenger for you with the other parent. It is your job to communicate with your ex-spouse, not your children's. They should not be put in the position of transferring things (money, paperwork, personal possessions, and legal documents, etc.) between the two of you, relaying information about changes in parenting schedules, or explaining an opinion about something. Anything that you might need to give or to say to your ex-spouse is your responsibility and should not be a burden placed on your children.

Always Provide Comfort and Support

You need to provide comfort to your children when they are missing the other parent. Be sensitive to the fact that they will always be missing one of you as they live in two homes, and this is a very difficult thing for them to cope with. Give them ample opportunity to talk about the challenges that this poses for them and be empathic in your responses to them. Support their having contact with the other parent by whatever means is comfortable for them (i.e., phone, FaceTime/Skype/Zoom, texting).

Create Peaceful Transitions

Try to make the pick-up and drop-off transitions as peaceful and calm as possible. These transitions are already very stressful for children and your job is not to add to this stress in any way. This is not the time for contentious conversations between the parents. It is also not helpful to set rules for the other parent that the children are required to enforce, and which subsequently result in them feeling uncomfortable. For example, it is not helpful to forbid your ex-spouse from parking in your driveway or ringing your doorbell because you want to minimize your contact with them. This only serves to create stress for your child and communicate your disdain for their other parent. This is one of those times that you need to rise above your feelings and put your children's needs/feelings first.

A personal anecdote might be useful to demonstrate how conflicting this can be for a child. The fact that I remember it so vividly after so many decades speaks to how upsetting it was for me at the time. After a visit with my dad, he asked if he could use the bathroom in the house before driving home. I was aware of my mom's rule that he wasn't allowed in the house, but it seemed absurd to not allow him in to use the bathroom if it was necessary, and I would clearly feel horrible about saying no. So, given that my mom wasn't home, I told him that he could come in. He proceeded to use the bathroom in the master bedroom (which was natural for him given that it used to be his bathroom) and he then went home. I assumed that my mom would never even know. Was I wrong! My dad apparently left the toilet seat up so when my mom went in to use her bathroom, she went ballistic! At first, I tried to deny letting him into the house (I was a teenager, so this came naturally), but she confronted me with the irrefutable evidence of the raised toilet seat, and I had no option but to confess my misdeed. I was put in the horrible position of needing to enforce a rule that made no sense to me and seemed to unnecessarily punish my father while at the same time knowing that I was betraying my mother if I chose to disregard her wishes.

Keep Children Out of Adult Conflicts

Do not use your child as a weapon or a pawn against the other parent. This happens far too frequently given the pain and anger that one or both parents may be experiencing during and post-divorce. It may be tempting to get back at your ex-spouse by trying to hurt them through the children, but you will inevitably be hurting the children as well. This can first become an issue during the decision-making process about custody. For example, a wounded parent may want to fight for full custody as a means of punishing a spouse for their infidelity. However, custody decisions should be based solely upon what is in the child's best interest, rather than on how pay-back can be best accomplished. This can also happen more subtly as the co-parenting relationship progresses. For example, one parent continuously creates scheduling conflicts that interfere with the children seeing the other parent at the scheduled times. While this will clearly be upsetting for the affected parent, it will also be causing your child to be needlessly upset. This needs to be avoided at all costs.

Minimize Differences between Homes

Try to maintain as much consistency as possible between the children's two homes. While you probably have different ideas about parenting and don't always see eye to eye about child-rearing strategies, there are typically many things that you can and should try to agree upon for your children's sake. For your youngest children, try to maintain as much consistency as possible between your two households with feeding/sleep schedules and toilet training strategies. With your older children, it will be extremely helpful to have consistent rules and expectations regarding homework time, limits on screen time, bedtime, grades, and social interactions. Doing so will minimize the amount of splitting that happens (i.e., pitting one parent against the other) and testing of the limits, especially in the house with the stricter parent ("Why can't I do that here when I am able to do it at daddy's house?").

Maintain Consistency

Do not try to prove that you are the better parent by being overly permissive or indulgent. It may be tempting to try to heal your children's divorce-related wounds by loosening up on previously established rules/expectations or becoming excessive with gifts or special events. This may be even more true if your children are angry with you for behavior that they believe resulted in the divorce (such as an affair). However tempting as this might be, what your children need most now is actually the exact opposite. They are in need of you expressing your love and continued care for them by means of you maintaining predictability, consistency, boundaries, and structure in their lives.

Stick to the Schedule

Strive to be extremely consistent in your parenting time schedule and avoid cancelling or postponing visits if at all possible. Your children have already experienced so much turmoil, instability, and loss through the divorce process. Consequently, your goal now needs to be to spare them any unnecessary unpredictability, inconsistency, or perceived loss/abandonment. They need to count on you to be where you said you would be and when you said you would be there. If for some you reason you are delayed or your plans have changed, it is important to make sure that your children know as soon as possible about these changes, and how this will impact your plans with them.

EFFECTIVE COMMUNICATION

In addition to these guidelines, the other most important component of being good co-parents is the ability to effectively communicate with each other. I often tell parents to think about this relationship as if it is a business relationship and to communicate with your ex-spouse as you would with a business associate (even if it is a co-worker that you don't particularly like). In those professional interactions your communication would most often be polite, respectful, non-emotional, and focused upon the business at hand. You would not be contentious, argumentative, verbally abusive, or personally demeaning. If you disagreed on something, you would work together to create consensus. As co-parents, your business is your children, their needs must be your priority, and you need to strive to talk to each other calmly, openly, and with mutual respect. When disagreements arise, which they inevitably will, make an appointment to talk to each other when the children are not around (rather than during drop-offs or pick-ups when the children are present) or seek out the help of a therapist or co-parenting coach to help you resolve your issues with each other.

Some of the most important things that you need to effectively communicate about include:

- Details about medical issues, school activities, and other important events
- Specifics about schedules, plans, or particular requests
- Particular behavioral or emotional issues that a child is having at home or at school
- Major decisions that need to be made regarding your child's life (health, education, religion)
- Any changes in your life that may have an emotional impact on your child (new relationships, re-marriage, birth of a child, loss of job)

Being able to talk to each other about these things will serve multiple purposes. It will ensure that the complicated details of children living within two homes will run as smoothly as possible. It will prevent things from falling through the cracks and parents not being aware of significant happenings in the children's lives. It will give each of you input into important decisions regarding your children. It will allow each of you to address any problems that have arisen in their lives. It will prevent the children from pitting the two of you against each other since you will both always be aware of their current struggles.

It will be important for you to jointly determine which mode of communication works best for the two of you (in person, phone, text, email) and then to consistently utilize that mode for the agreed upon reasons. For example, you may agree to always either talk in person or by phone for important medical issues but to utilize texting for scheduling issues.

Whatever you decide, the plan should be specific and adhered to consistently. There are some great online tools available to help facilitate the necessary sharing of important information. For example, Our Family Wizard is an app developed specifically to help parents coordinate their parenting schedule, facilitate making changes to that schedule, manage shared financial expenses, and organize their communication with each other in one secure place. Other similar apps include 2houses, Talking Parents, Coparently, and Cozi (whose basic app is free with upgrades available for a fee). Please go to the Resources link at childcentereddivorcejourney.com to get more information on these various co-parenting apps.

It is also important to have realistic expectations about your post-divorce communication with your ex-spouse. It is probably safe to assume that the two of you struggled in the past to effectively communicate with each other and that one or both of you had limitations in your ability to express yourself to your spouse that contributed to these issues. It is also safe to assume that these same issues will persist into your post-marriage life and will pose challenges in your ability to co-parent together. Adhering to the guidelines and suggestions above will help you compensate for these deficits and challenges and provide you with the tools necessary to raise your children together in the best possible manner.

Another very important piece of advice that I always give to co-parents is **not to assume malicious intent**. What I mean by this is to strive to give the other parent the benefit of the doubt and not to jump automatically to the conclusion that they are somehow attempting to hurt you, not being honest, or intentionally trying to make your life miserable. It is easy to assume malicious intent when you have previously been hurt by that person's prior behavior, but it can also frequently be a faulty assumption that unnecessarily leads to conflict and tension. I see it happen frequently in my practice, and it can cause unnecessary conflict and anger. Work hard to accept what your ex-spouse is saying without guessing that they really mean something else. Clarify with them what they are trying to communicate, rather than simply assuming and reacting based upon that assumption. Try to accept their intentions at face value rather than presuming that there is an underlying motive to do something evil toward you. Once again, this will not be easy, but working toward this goal will have huge payoffs in terms of your co-parenting relationship.

HOW TO DO IT BETTER

Amy and Charlie divorced after sixteen years of marriage. They have two children, Evan who is fourteen and Sarah who is eleven. The last few years of their marriage were very difficult and were full of conflict and tension. They worked very hard to not fight in front of the children but were not always successful. While they were both often tempted to try to enlist their children's support in their arguments, they tried to avoid that from happening, again not always successfully. At least they were making the effort.

It was important for both of them to remain actively involved in their children's lives post-divorce, so they agreed to share legal and physical custody. They developed a parenting plan that gave them close to equal amounts of time with the children each week. Given Amy's frequent work travel, they built in some flexibility so that Charlie would be able to have the children when she was not available. Given their history of difficulty communicating, they decided to utilize Our Family Wizard as a means of sharing information with each other about the children's schedules. They also agreed that they would phone or text each other when there were important decisions to be made. This became necessary shortly after the divorce was final. Evan was at soccer practice with Charlie when he fell and badly hurt his ankle. On the way to the hospital, Charlie called Amy, told her what had happened, and she arrived at the ER shortly after they did. Charlie and Amy were both there to support Evan and to make the important medical decisions regarding his care. Evan couldn't have felt more loved by both of his parents than he did at that moment.

Several months later, Charlie and Amy had a huge disagreement about money, and it started to spill over onto the children. The transition times became very stressful for them since their parents were being nasty toward each other. Communication started to break down and Charlie and Amy began using the children to relay messages. Scheduling mishaps became more frequent and everyone was getting increasingly frustrated. Evan and Sarah finally had enough and decided to talk to each of their parents about how horrible things had become for them since the money fight. Charlie and Amy were horrified about the impact that their conflict was having on their children. They set up a time to talk when the children were not around and worked to resolve the financial issue that originally caused the fight. They also re-committed to not allowing their issues with each other to negatively impact the children as they had been doing over the past month. They sat down together with both children and praised them for having the courage to come to them with this concern and promised to work their hardest to not let this happen again.

This story illustrates that co-parenting will not always be easy and that there will be frequent challenges that you will face. You will not do it perfectly all the time and that should clearly not be your expectation. A more realistic goal will be to work as hard as you can to incorporate as many of the suggestions that I have detailed into your co-parenting relationship. It is going to take a tremendous amount of discipline and emotional control and you will not always be successful. Refer back to the chapter on how to best cope with your stress frequently. I can promise that giving it your best effort will have a huge positive impact on your children's post-divorce functioning and will minimize the chances of them developing more serious problems as they work their way through the divorce process.

1 2

DATING AND THE INTRODUCTION OF NEW SIGNIFICANT OTHERS TO YOUR CHILDREN

S tarting to date again is often one of the next steps in the divorce journey and one which can either be done well or can be done poorly and can potentially cause further emotional pain for everyone involved. The following scenarios exemplify some of the common mistakes that parents make when they venture back into the world of dating.

Case 1

Paula had engaged in an extra-marital affair with Ted for years before her husband eventually found out about it and initiated a divorce. Her husband was so enraged by the betrayal that he inappropriately shared details about it with their twelve-year-old daughter Alice. As a result, Alice hated Ted before ever meeting him and blamed him for ending her parent's marriage. Shortly after Paula moved out of the family home, she decided that it was time for Alice to meet Ted given that he had become such an important part of her life. Despite Alice's reluctance, the initial meeting took place and Alice immediately decided that she hated Ted and wanted nothing to do with him. Paula, however, felt that her daughter was simply being defiant, so she continued to include Ted in all of her visits with Alice. Their relationship became so strained that now Alice not only hated Ted but started to hate her mom as well.

Case 2

Nancy divorced less than a year ago and decided that she was ready to start dating. She utilized several online dating sites and started meeting men fairly regularly. She believed that her children, ages nine and eleven, should have input on whether she remained in a relationship on more than a casual basis. So, after two months of dating Hal, she brought him home to meet the children. They both seemed to hit it off with him, so she felt as if she had gotten their blessing to continue in the relationship. The four of them spent increasing amounts of time together, and the children started to get very attached to him. After several more months of dating, Nancy started to see things in Hal that she didn't like and decided to end the relationship. The children were devastated! They had just started to get used to there being another man in their lives and now he was gone. To make it worse, their mom told them that they would probably never see him again.

Case 3

Bob divorced ten months ago and had shared custody of his ten- and thirteen-year-old children, Mike and Deirdre. He started dating Fran a month ago, and they were spending increasing amounts of time together. She had two children the same age as Bob's, and they both badly wanted the children to meet each other in order to see how they would mesh. Both of them were warned by friends and family to not prematurely involve the children in their relationship. In order to heed that warning, they decided to set up an "accidental" meeting at the local ice-cream parlor. When they ran into each other the following weekend, Bob introduced Fran as a friend from work. They hung out together while eating their ice-cream and the kids seemed to get along well. Two weeks later, they "ran into" each other again at the miniature golf range and played their round together. Mike and Deirdre were getting suspicious about these supposedly accidental meetings and the way in which their dad and Fran seemed very flirty with each other. When they came home from their dad's, they told their mom about his friend Fran who they kept running into. Their mom started crying and blurted out that Fran is not his friend but is the woman he has been dating for the past several months. The children felt angry and betrayed and started wondering what other things their dad had been lying about to them.

These three stories are unfortunately very typical and reflect some of the common mistakes that parents can make as they start to date. Let me detail some guidelines that will hopefully help you avoid these and other missteps and, consequently, spare your children any additional instability and emotional pain beyond that which the divorce may have already caused.

SOME KEY GUIDELINES

Maintain Boundaries

Keep your dating life separate from your relationship with your children. It is "adult business" that they do not need to be part of. Ideally, do your dating on nights that the children are not with you (assuming that you are sharing custody with the other parent). Do not invite someone to your house after your children fall asleep because they will inevitably wake up and wonder who the stranger is in their home. Do not "sneak out" after they go to bed given the potential for them waking and finding a babysitter in the house that they did not expect to be there.

Give It Time

It is crucially important that significant others not be introduced to the children until the relationship is long-term and committed. Parents often ask for a specific timeframe (how many months does it have to be?) and my answer is that it is really more of a qualitative than a quantitative issue. What you are trying to avoid is prematurely involving somebody in your children's lives, your children then becoming attached to that person, and the relationship then ending. It takes many months (if not years) to really get to know someone, to be secure in the type of person that they are, and to be confident in the potential for the relationship to endure. Until that happens, the children should not be part of that relationship. It is okay for you to share with your curious older children that you are starting to date, but make clear to them that you will not be sharing details with them about these relationships. Your primary goal needs to be sparing your children any additional loss, grief, or instability given how much they have already experienced due to the divorce. You should err on the side of caution and not make this about your needs (i.e., "it would be so much easier if I didn't have to keep these relationships separate, I am so curious to find out what my children think of my new significant other and what he/she will be like with my children"). There will be a time and place for this to happen, but hopefully not until there is minimal chance that the relationship is going to end. I have seen far too many children exposed to a revolving door of parental dating relationships that result in a constant state of loss, abandonment, and grief for their children. The purpose of this guideline is to hopefully prevent that from happening to your children.

Inform the Other Parent

Once you have determined that it is an appropriate time to introduce your new significant other to the children, it is important to inform the other parent that this is going to happen prior to the meeting. This is a significant event in your children's lives and is therefore something that the other parent should be made aware of. This will allow them to be able to support the children in adjusting to this new reality in their lives. It should not be kept a secret, especially one that the children are expected to keep from the other parent. The openness about this between parents also communicates to the children that their parents will always work together to help them deal with changes in their lives. Often, the ex-spouse requests an opportunity to meet the new significant other prior to the children meeting him/her. I think this is a perfectly reasonable request and one that should be honored. That person is presumably going to play a significant role in the children's lives and such an introduction could lay the groundwork for a healthy relationship among the significant adults in your children's lives.

Give Children Permission to Develop New Relationships

One of the greatest gifts that you can give your child at this time is the permission to have a positive, loving relationship with your ex's significant other. Making explicit statements such as "it is okay to like mommy's new boyfriend" or "it will make me happy if you enjoy spending time with your dad's new girlfriend" will free your children up to establish a happy healthy relationship with this new person in their life and not have to worry that doing so will upset or hurt their other parent. Doing this step right can create the foundation for a lifetime of comfortable interactions between all of you, whereas doing this poorly can be the start of years of conflicted loyalties, tense relationships, and immeasurable amounts of stress for everyone involved. If necessary, consider it another business relationship that you need to work on to foster.

Don't Rush the Relationship

Another important ground rule is to give your child time to slowly develop a relationship with your significant other. That person is a stranger to them, despite the fact that they are intimately involved with you. You need to provide the time and space necessary for the relationship to slowly evolve rather than attempt to foist it on your children. Support them spending fun time together sharing an activity that they all enjoy, either with or without you. I have seen the attempt to push the relationship too quickly backfire far too many times, resulting in negative feelings toward either the parent or their new partner, so I caution you on making that same mistake.

Preserve Quality Time with Your Children

It is important that not all of your time with your children is spent with your new partner. They will inevitably feel jealous and threatened of the time that you are spending with this person and may fear losing you to them. It is crucial that you reassure them that this will never happen, both through your words and your actions. It will be important that you try to establish special time with each child as well as time for you as a nuclear unit (without the significant other) as a means of demonstrating this. This may not be what you are wanting now, but it is clearly what your children will be needing.

Maintain Roles

Do not allow your new partner to take on a parental role with your children at this time (or anytime soon). It is not appropriate for them to start disciplining your children, establishing new rules, or changing rules that previously existed. This will only lead to anger and resentment toward that person and will interfere in the development of a positive relationship with your children. You are the parent and you need to maintain that role and not delegate it to your new partner.

Be Patient

Expect resistance from your children as a normal part of this transition. Try not to respond to this with anger but rather with understanding and compassion. This can be a very challenging and scary time for your children and approaching it with patience and support will go a long way toward helping them successfully negotiate their way through it.

A BETTER WAY OF DOING IT

Susan and Ron divorced several years ago and have a nine-year-old daughter Jessica. Susan started dating Scott five months ago and is starting to really like him. She badly wants Jessica to meet him, both to get her approval as well as to see what Scott is like when he interacts with her. Susan's therapist has warned her that it is probably too soon to introduce them, so she decides to hold off on doing so for at least another four or five months. Jessica has started to get suspicious that her mom has a new boyfriend and has begun asking questions about him. Susan honestly tells her that she does have a new friend who she is spending time with, but that this is adult business that she is not going to be discussing in detail with her at this time.

Six months later, Susan and Scott are still dating, and their relationship has gotten more serious. They are starting to talk about moving in together and possibly getting married sometime soon after. Susan feels like it is now the right time to introduce Scott to her daughter. She decides to give Ron a call to let him know about the seriousness of her relationship with Scott and her readiness to introduce him to their daughter. Ron requests that he be given the opportunity to meet Scott since he will be spending a lot of time with their daughter. Susan is initially reluctant to do this since it reminds her of previous times when Ron tried to control her life. However, after discussing this with her therapist, she decides that she would want the same opportunity if Ron was seriously dating someone and that it was therefore a reasonable request. They set up the meeting and, despite it being terribly uncomfortable, it felt like it was the right thing to do.

Several weeks later, Susan invites Scott over for dinner to meet Jessica. While she was terribly nervous about how things would go, the two of them really seemed to hit it off. Susan was thrilled and felt that they could now start doing everything together as a new family. It quickly became clear that this was pushing things way too fast for Jessica. She started acting out every time Scott came over, doing all sorts of inappropriate things to get Susan's attention. In an attempt to support Susan, Scott tried to discipline Jessica for her inappropriate behavior. This only served to make things worse since now Jessica was getting angry at Scott. At one point she yelled at him that "you're not my father and you can't tell me what to do." Susan realized that things were starting to spiral out of control and that she needed to slow things down and give Jessica time to establish her own relationship with Scott. She also clearly told Scott that it was her job to discipline her child, not his, and that he needed to refrain from doing so.

After this re-set, things started going much better. Susan spent a good deal of time alone with Jessica during her visitation time and maybe an hour or two per week together with Scott doing something fun. Jessica was slowly able to establish a relationship with him that did not involve him being in a parental role. She started to really enjoy their time together, began to actually look forward to it, and eventually started to ask her mom for it to happen more often.

The process of introducing new partners into your children's lives needs to be handled with sensitivity and patience. It is very important that their emotional needs during this time are put above your own in order to avoid causing them any additional unnecessary pain. If done well, this can be a wonderful time of healing, excitement, and new beginnings. It can bring new love into your life and the lives of your children.

13

REMARRIAGE AND THE
BLENDED FAMILY

Research shows that it can take up to five years for new families to fully blend. This suggests that this process needs to slowly evolve over time and cannot be pushed or hurried. Everyone involved, adults and children, must be sensitized to this fact and accept the need to be patient with the process. Like every previous step in the divorce journey, there are ways to do this well and there are many mistakes that can be made that have the potential to damage emotionally both you and your children. The goal of this chapter is to lay out strategies to help you do this right. When you do so, this can be the start of a wonderfully happy new phase in your divorce journey. You can do this!

There are many challenges that each new blended family will face and potential solutions for best managing or resolving each of those challenges.

THE PROCESS OF BLENDING FAMILIES

Respecting the Grieving Process

Most, if not all, family members have experienced the loss of a relationship prior to the establishment of this new family (either through death or divorce). Therefore, you are all probably still dealing with some aspect of the grieving process which will have an impact on your willingness and comfort level to enter into new relationships. Each person will need to be given the time that they need to feel safe and allow themselves to be vulnerable again.

Honoring and Blending Lifestyles

Every family has its own unique lifestyle and way of doing things. Blending two families, therefore, poses the specific challenge of figuring out how to create a new lifestyle that respects and incorporates each family's old way of doing things. Finding the balance between holding onto some of the familiarity of the past while establishing a new blended lifestyle is the goal at this time. It requires a great deal of dialogue, mutual respect, and patience from every family member to do this successfully.

Negotiation and Compromise about Parenting Styles

There are many challenges related to power and authority with newly blended families. The parents need to determine how they are going to deal with their differing parenting styles and what their roles will be with their new partner's children. This is often the area in which the greatest mistakes are made. It is very common at this time for the stricter parent to step in and try to establish new rules and expectations for the other parent's children. This inevitably results in anger and resentment for both the children and their parent as well as conflict between the two adults. It is very important for each parent to maintain their role as the primary disciplinarian for their own children. It is also going to be necessary for the adults to negotiate a set of mutually agreed upon family rules and expectations and to slowly incorporate them into the children's lives. Immediately trying to impose a whole new set of rules for the children will inevitably result in anger and resentment for them and may serve to poison their relationship with both the stepparent as well as their biological parent. It will probably also result in a lot of conflict with your new spouse. You need to respect your spouse's history with his/her children and not try to impose your parenting style. It will take time, effort, and patience to negotiate a common set of parenting principles that you can both embrace.

Establishing New Roles

Everyone may be feeling confused about their new family roles. Children are often experiencing confusion about the role that their new stepparent is going to be playing in their life. They may also be unclear about the nature of their relationship with new stepsiblings. At the same time, the adults are trying to figure out what their roles should be with their new stepchildren as well as in their new shared role as head of this newly blended family. This role confusion can be very stressful for everyone involved and must be acknowledged and addressed openly, honestly, thoughtfully, and frequently. Establishing a new set of family roles takes time and requires a great deal of patience and hard work. Trust me, in the end it will be worth all of the effort that you put into it!

Managing Conflicting Loyalties

This is often the time when conflicting loyalties and allegiances become problematic. The children may be struggling with guilt about establishing a loving relationship with a new stepparent. For example, they may feel disloyal to their dad if they start feeling close to their stepdad or that they are betraying their mom if they enjoy doing things with their stepmom. Parents often either subtly or overtly contribute to this guilt by their words or actions. They may remind their children that "you only have one mother" or "he is not your dad, remember that!" As I stated in a previous chapter, giving your children permission to have a close loving relationship with their new stepparent is one of the greatest gifts you can give them at this time. It will free them up to establish a healthy relationship with their new stepparent while at the same time maintaining a positive relationship with their biological parents. You need to trust that you can never be replaced as your child's parent, regardless of how much they love their new stepparent.

Adjusting to Changing Family Structure

Another potential challenge for children as families blend is the change in their ordinal (youngest, middle, oldest) position in the family. For example, your daughter may have been the "baby" in your family, but she will now become the middle child in the newly blended family given that your new spouse has a younger son. This can be disorienting for the children since it can change their own self-perception as well as the way in which they are treated by others. This is not something that can be avoided but it must be an issue that you are all aware of and sensitive to. Giving your children frequent opportunities to talk about the emotional impact that this change is having on them is crucial at this time.

Maintaining Alone Time with Children

Children can become very worried about whether their parent is going to have enough time and love left for them given all of the new competing relationships. They might start resenting the time that their parent spends with the new spouse or stepchildren. They could start acting out as a means of getting negative attention which they might perceive as preferable to no attention at all. It is important to be proactive about this and create frequent and predictable times that you and your biological children can have special time together (and your spouse can do the same with his/her children). It is essential to nourish this relationship at this time when your children are feeling that it is most threatened.

Accepting Parents Will Never Reconcile

As we discussed previously, children can hold onto fantasies of reconciliation for many years. The re-marriage of a parent presents a stark reality that this is not going to happen and that their parents are never going to be together again. As a result, this transition can trigger an increase in sadness and grief in a child. It is important to be aware of this possibility and to be there to emotionally support your child if it does occur, even when their grief is manifested as anger.

Allow Time for Relationships to Develop

Parents often unrealistically expect that there will be instant love among the new family members. They hope that their children will love the new stepparent given that this is how they feel toward them. They want badly for the children to all get along and quickly develop a strong family bond. They expect that they will love their new spouse's children based upon their love of their spouse. Developing a true loving relationship takes time and cannot be forced or rushed. It must develop slowly, over time, and be built upon the foundation of many shared positive experiences. Attempting to force these relationships will inevitably backfire and doing so should be avoided.

Honoring the Biological Parents

It is important to always respect the fact that children only have one biological mother and one biological father and that nobody can or should try to replace that parent (except under certain unique circumstances such as when a biological parent dies when a child is very young, the surviving parent quickly remarries, and the stepparent is the only mom or dad that the child has ever known). Children should not be asked or required to refer to their stepparent as mom or dad when they already have a mother or father present in their life. That puts them in the uncomfortable position of feeling like they are betraying their biological parent and that needs to be avoided if at all possible.

Developing New Styles of Communication

Communication can often be a challenge in newly created blended families. The two families come into the relationship with differing histories of communication styles and rules and often struggle to create a new shared style of interacting with each other. It takes a lot of time and concerted effort to accomplish this and the parents need to be tasked with creating the proper environment for this to happen. Structuring weekly family meetings can be a powerful tool in fostering positive, open, and honest communication. Children and parents can both have input regarding issues of concern that they would like to discuss at the meeting and parents set the ground rules for respectful communication (everyone gets a chance to speak, no one can interrupt, everyone treats each other with respect, no hurtful or demeaning comments). This can be the time to openly discuss such topics as family rules, relationship challenges, expectations regarding chores, where to go on vacation.

It is also important to build some fun into these meetings. Perhaps they can end with a family activity that each child gets a chance to pick. The very act of regularly holding these meetings communicates that the parents deeply care about how their children are adjusting to this stressful new family dynamic, and that they are committed to doing everything possible to make this new family a happy and healthy one.

Adjusting to a New Baby

The birth of a new child into this blended family can be a source of distress for the existing children and can throw off the new and fragile equilibrium that has been created. They can feel threatened and displaced by the new baby who is now the only child who is fortunate enough to get to live with both of their biological parents. They can feel jealous of the attention that this child is getting from their parents and grandparents. They might feel resentful of being asked or required to take on caretaking responsibilities for the new baby (and parents need to be sensitive to this and not over-burden children with parental responsibilities). Again, it is essential that the children be given ample opportunity to talk about these feelings and feel heard and understood by both parents.

Maintaining Stability

As always, consistency and predictability are very important for your children during this time. Given that re-marriage may involve a physical move, try to keep your children in the same school district if at all possible. Try to avoid moving very far from their other parent which would serve to make the transitions between homes more stressful.

Given all of these challenges, I hope you can now see why it can take years for new stepfamilies to successfully blend. Hopefully, it is also clear that it is not just the passage of time that results in a healthy new family. It takes a lot of effort, work, patience, understanding, support, and love to successfully navigate your way through this major life transition. It can be done and can result in the start of a wonderful new chapter in your and your children's lives. Hopefully, you now have a clearer sense of the steps that you can take to get to this positive place in your divorce journey.

14

CONCLUSION

My assumption in writing this book and creating the website childcentereddivorcejourney.com is that you are about to embark on your own personal divorce journey or are already somewhere along the way. Given that, you probably have so many questions, so many difficult feelings, and a tremendous amount of concern about how you and your children are going to make it through this process. You must be overwhelmed with trying to figure out how this whole divorce process actually works. I'm sure you are scared about having to tell your children and terrified about how they are going to get through this ordeal. How will you help them, or yourself, if you start to really struggle? I'm sure you are starting to wonder how you and your soon to be ex-spouse will ever be able to work together to raise your children given that you are barely able to look at each other or be in the same room at this point. While dating and remarriage are probably nowhere on your radar yet, trust me, you will get there before you know it and some of those challenges may feel overwhelming as well.

My goal, first and foremost, in writing this book and creating childcentereddivorcejourney.com has been to give you hope. Hope that there is a way to get through this process healthy and emotionally intact. Hope that your children can get through it with some minor scars that can be fully healed. Hope that you can manage your stress and theirs in the best possible way. And, hope that there is a future waiting for you and your children that is full of new love and family harmony.

It can be done. My goal has been to provide you with a roadmap with very detailed suggestions and guidelines regarding how to work your way through this journey in the healthiest possible way for you and your entire family. It will, hopefully, serve as a step-by-step guide for what to do and not to do as you reach each step along the divorce journey. I have hope for you and for your children that you can do this well.

BEST OF LUCK ON YOUR JOURNEY!!!!!

THANK YOU FOR READING!

Please visit my website, childcentereddivorcejourney.com, or follow me on Instagram, Facebook, and Twitter for further information, resources, and support as you go through you own personal divorce journey.

Share what you thought!

ABOUT THE AUTHOR

D r. Erica Ellis is a licensed psychologist with over thirty years of experience treating children, adults, and families in her clinical practice. She has helped hundreds of families work their way through divorce and its aftermath. Dr. Ellis is also a Collaborative Divorce Coach and has received advanced training in matrimonial law and divorce mediation. Together with her legal colleagues, she has helped many divorcing couples successfully resolve their divorce without going to court. In addition to her clinical and collaborative work, Dr. Ellis has taught at the graduate level and has spoken locally, nationally, and internationally on the topic of divorce.

CPSIA information can be obtained
at www.ICGtesting.com
Printed in the USA
LVHW040100071020
668072LV00006B/664